*RuchiNisha Creations*

# Mindful Mandalas

## A Calming Colouring Journey

Mindful Colouring book for adults with 50 designs and thoughtful quotes!

*RuchiNisha Creations*

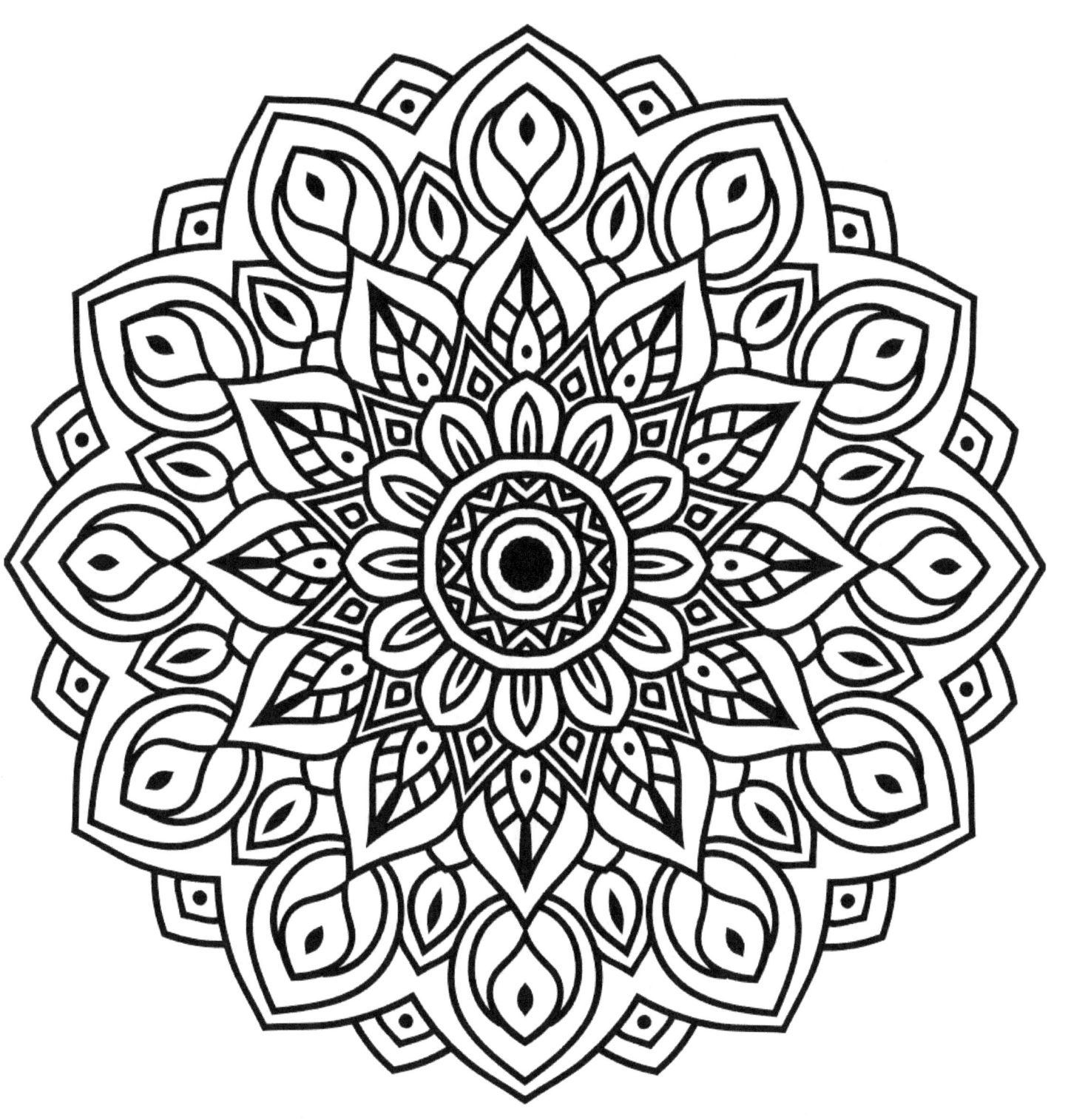

"The only way to achieve true happiness is to cherish what you have and forget what you don't have."

– Unknown

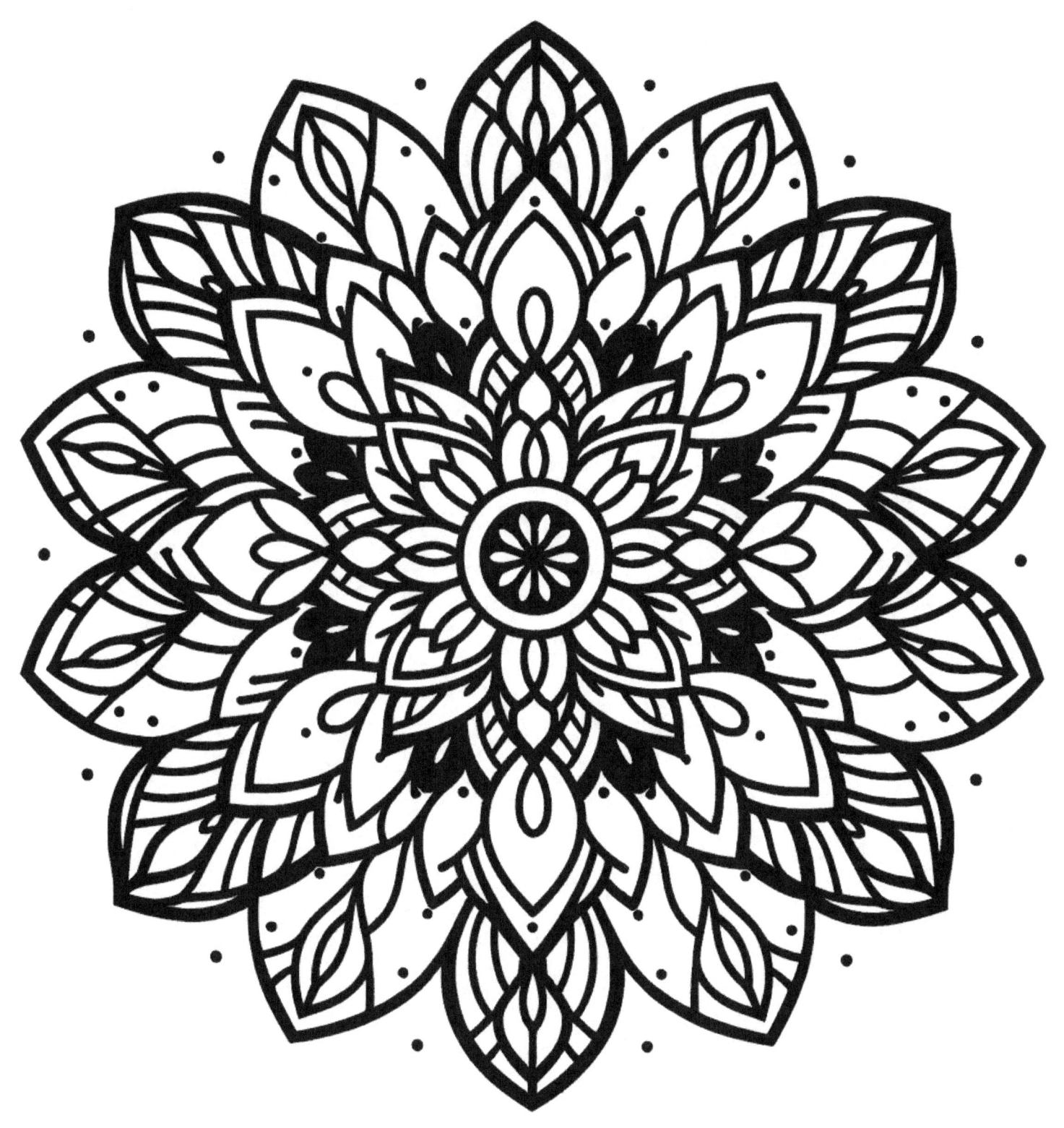

"There are far too many people that waste their time telling themselves that they don't have enough time."

– Unknown

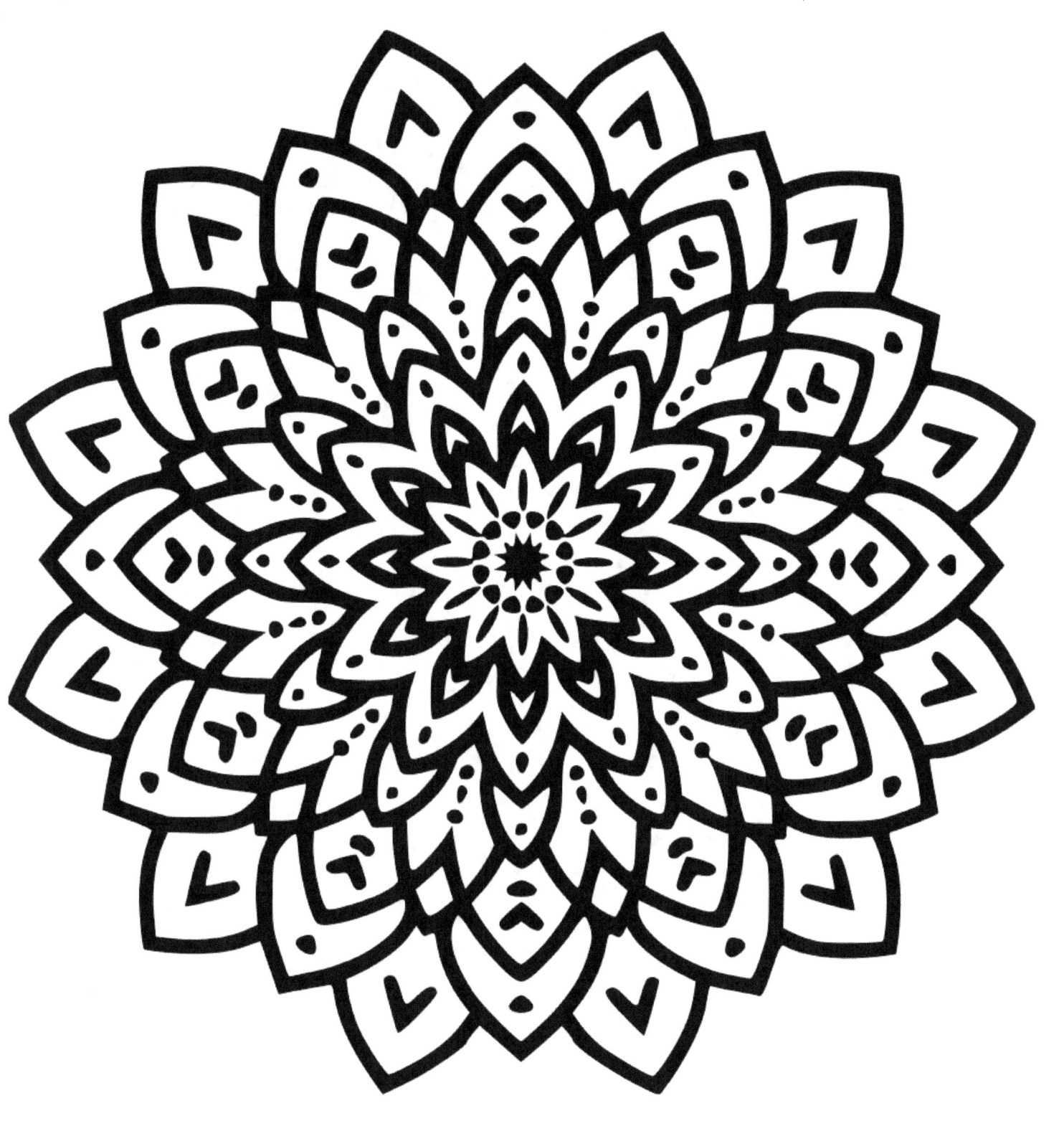

"Positivity is a choice. It's all about your perspective."

- Unknown

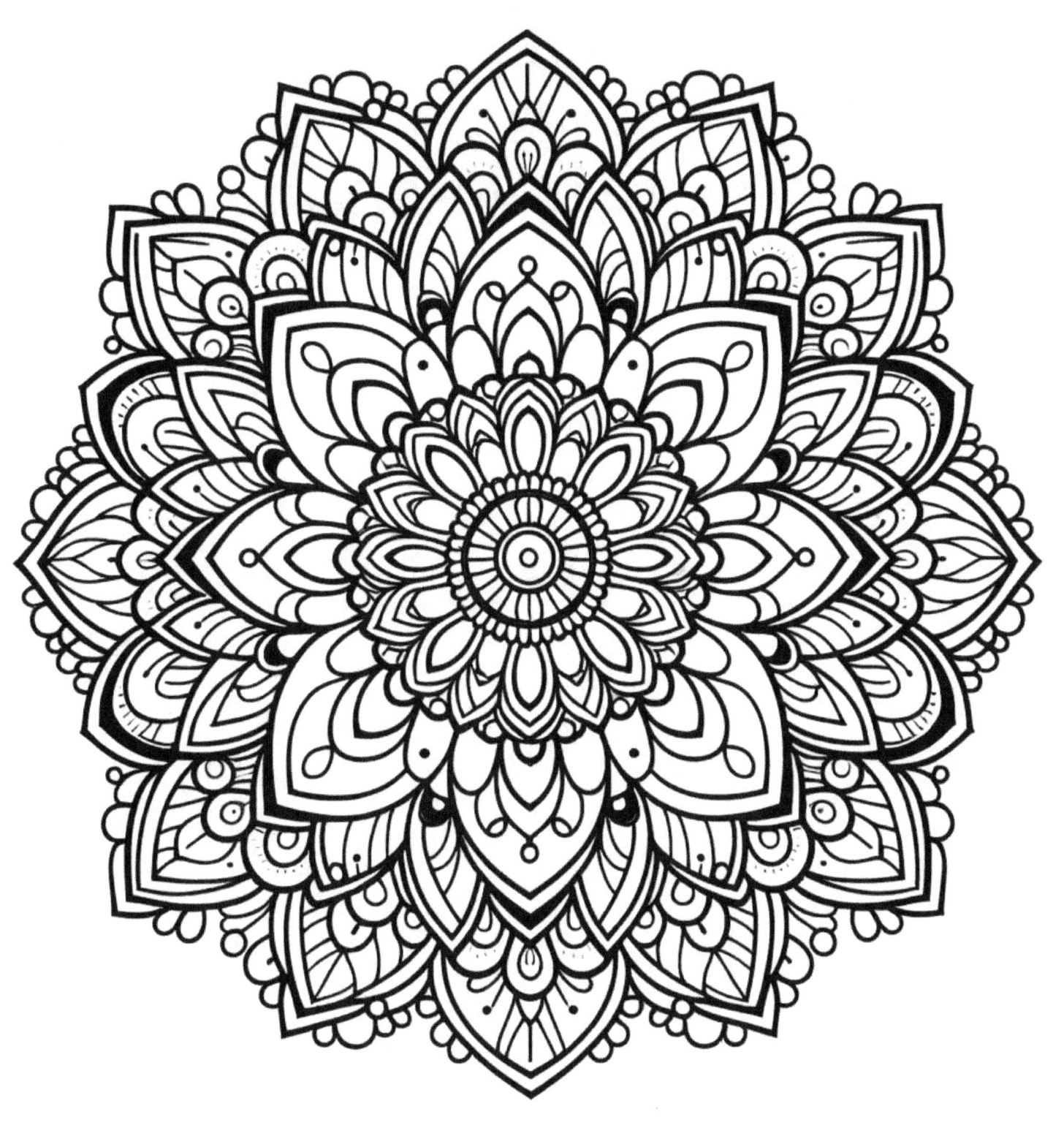

"A positive attitude will lead to positive outcomes."

– Unknown

"Train your mind to see the good in every situation."

– Unknown

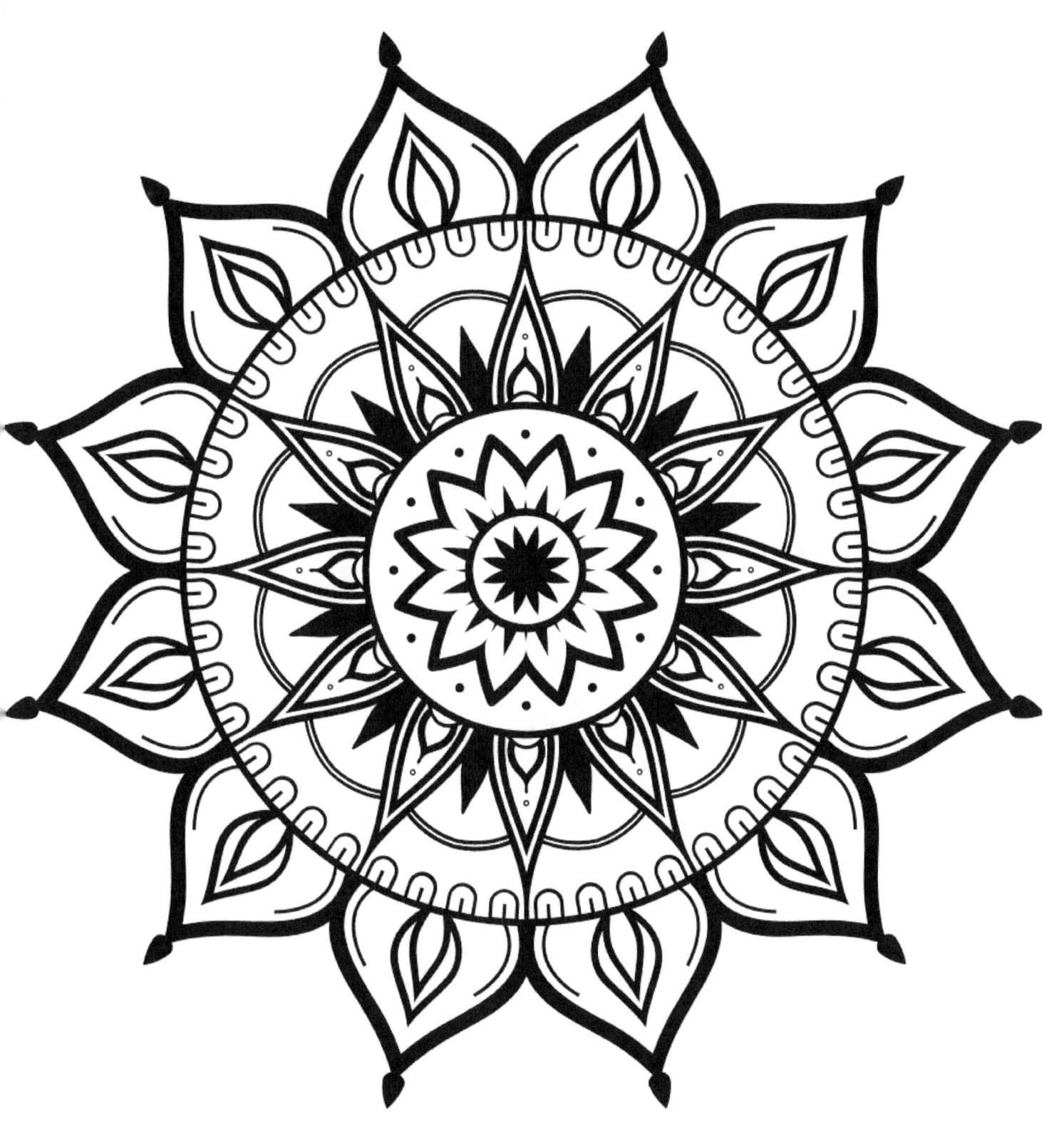

"At the end of the day, you can either focus on what's tearing you apart or what's holding you together."

– Unknown

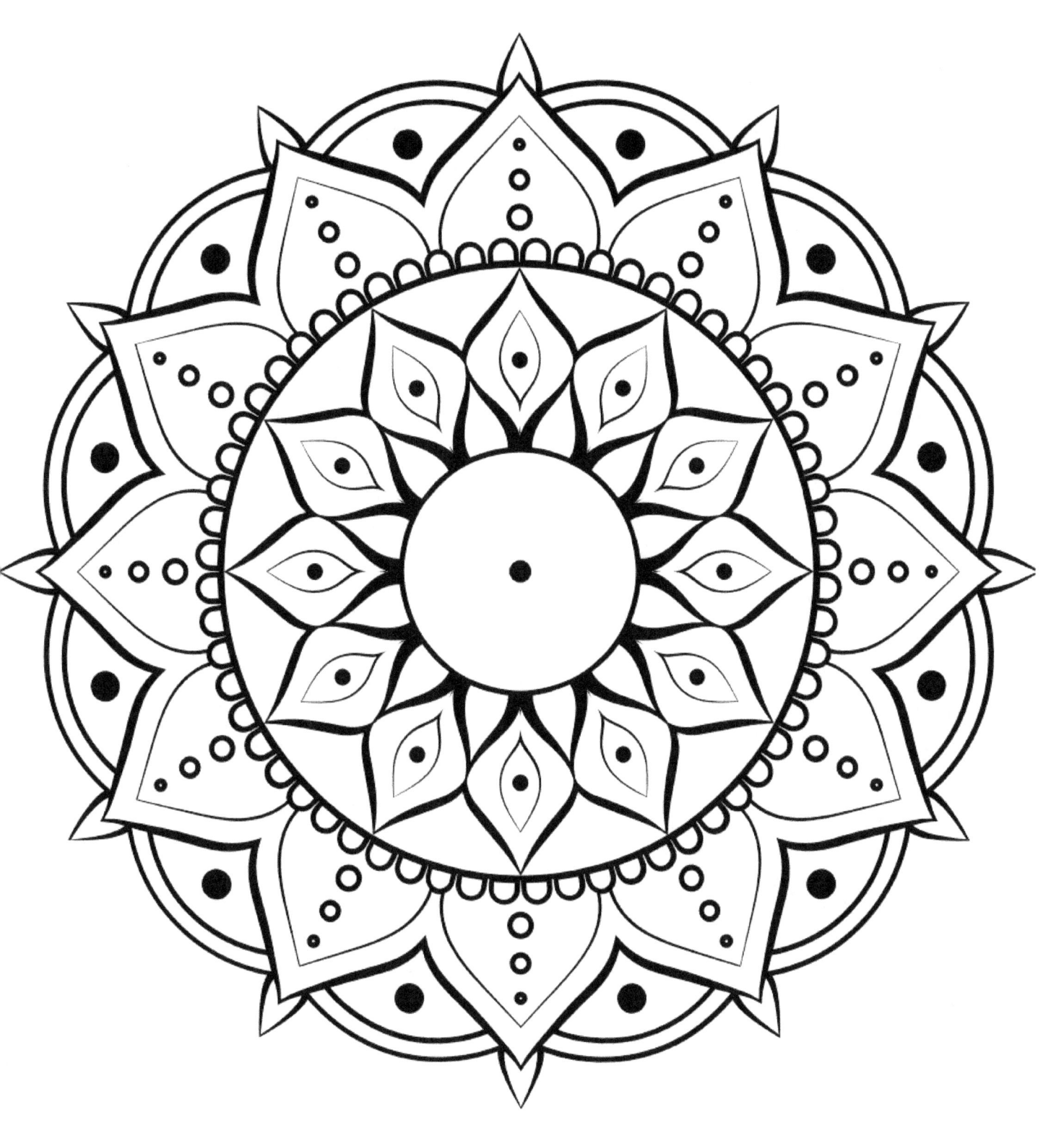

"Your attitude determines your direction."

– Unknown

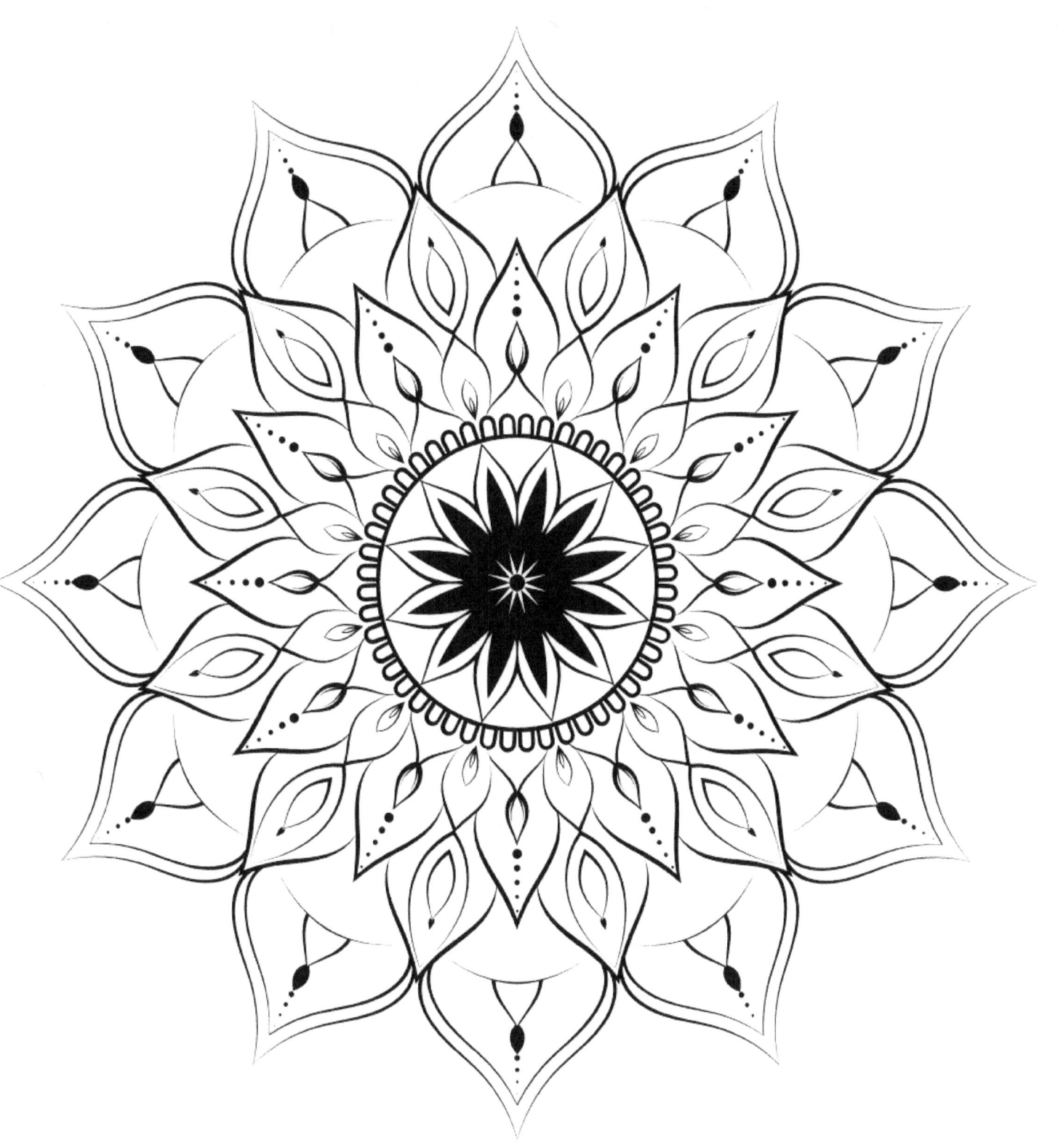

"Keep putting out good. It will come back to you tenfold in unexpected ways."

– Unknown

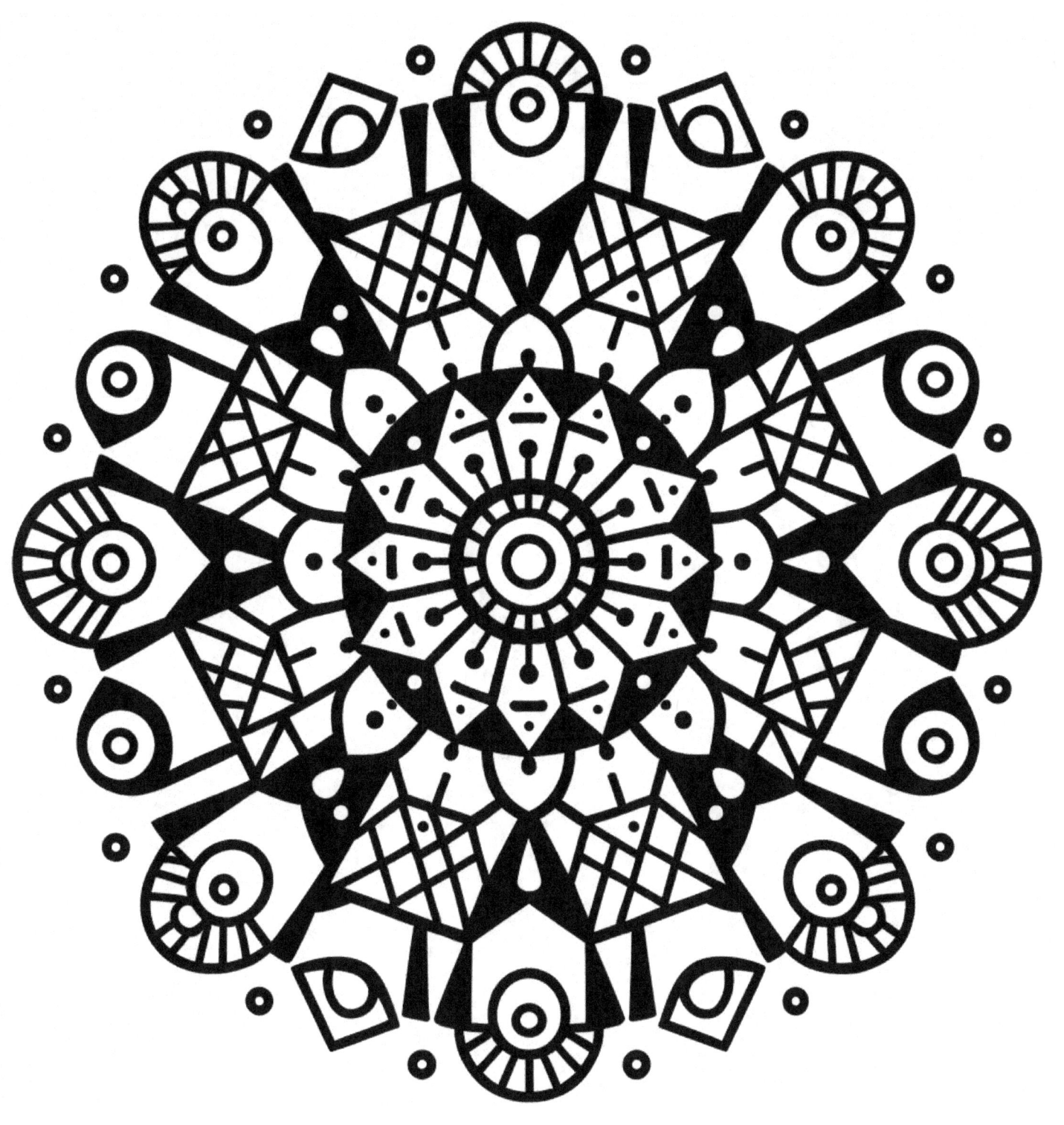

"Make your decisions out of love and kindness, and you will never regret any of them."

– Unknown

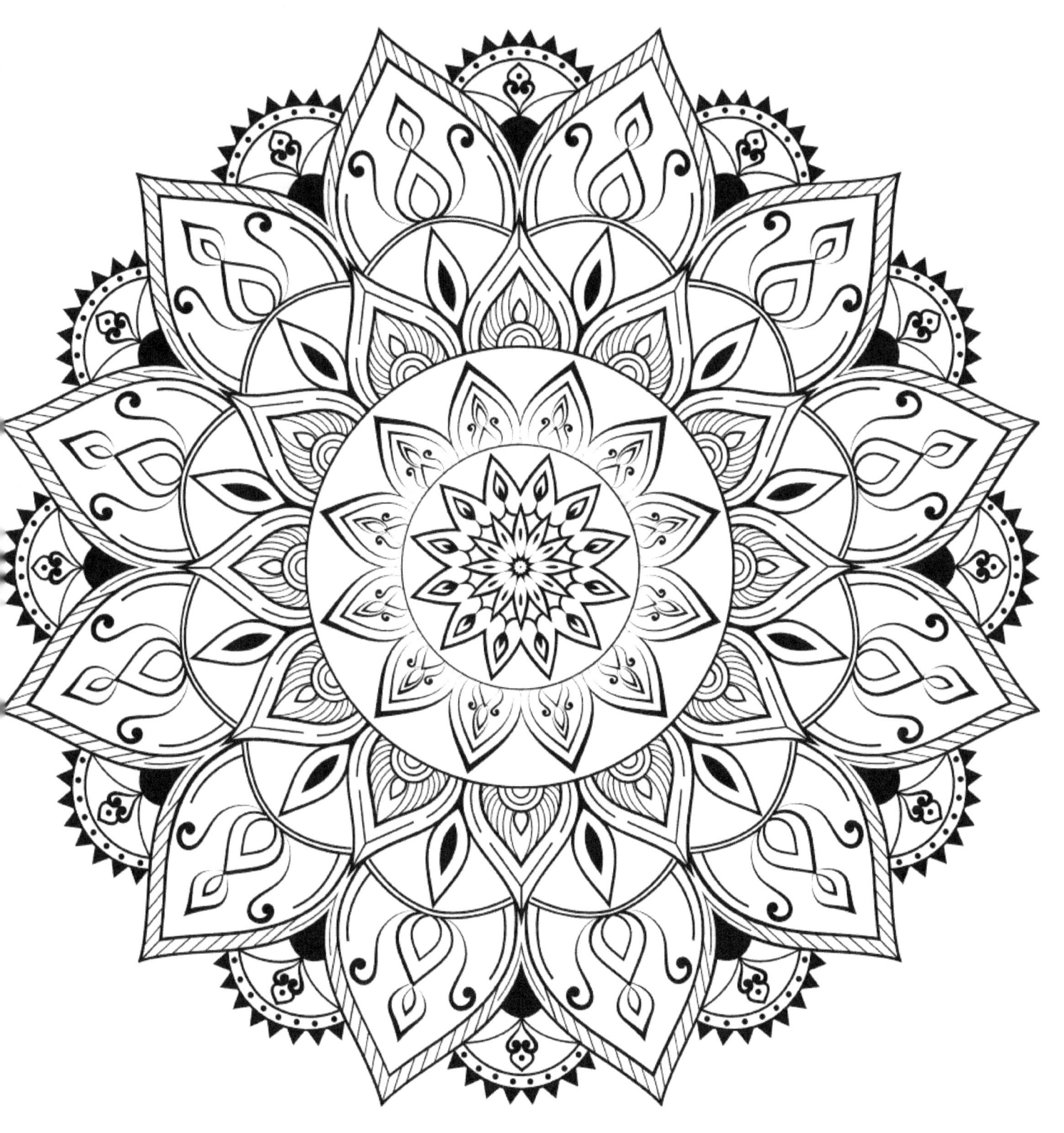

"Be the kind of person you want to meet."

- Unknown

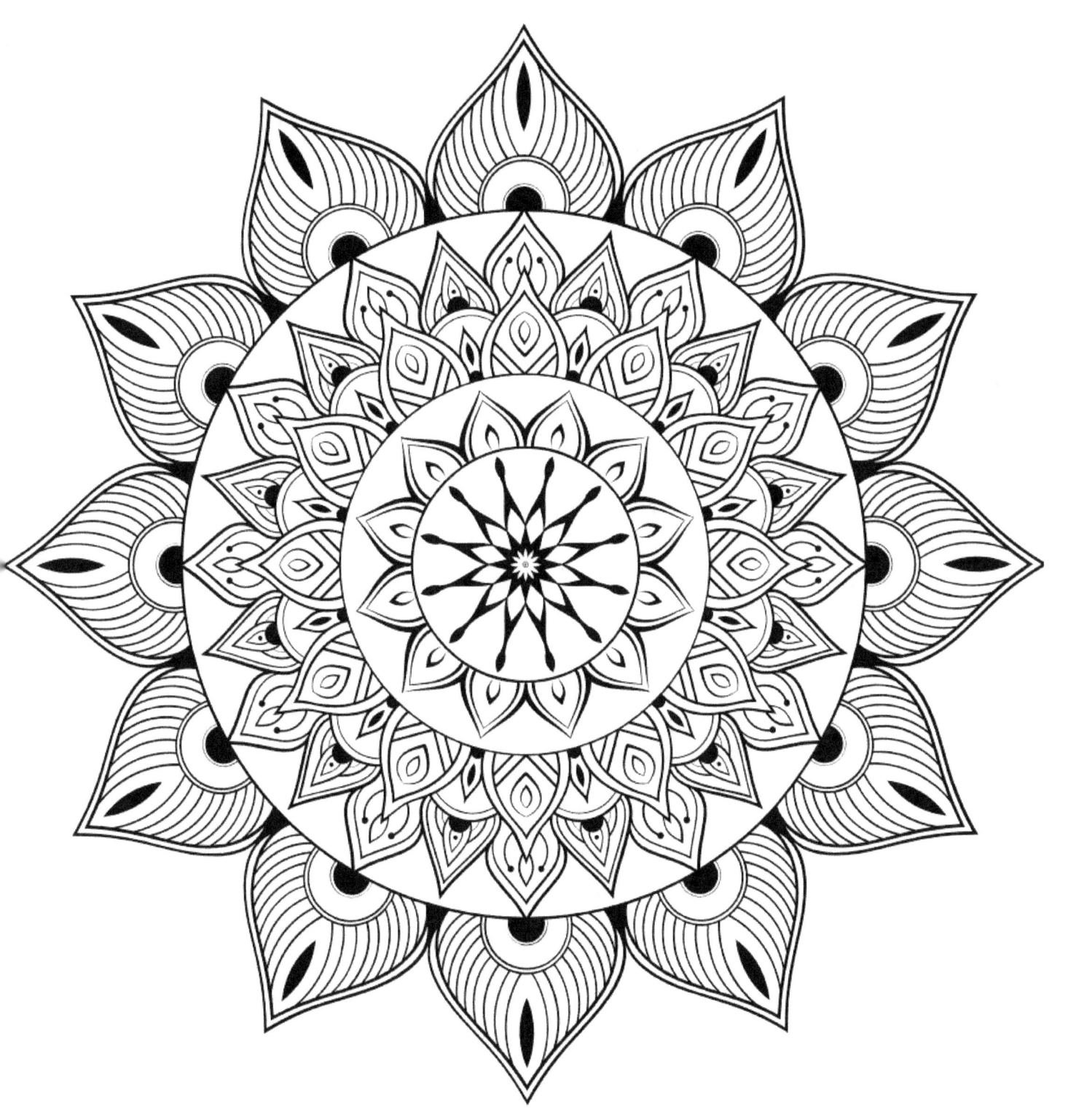

"Focus on the journey, not the destination. Joy is found not in finishing an activity but in doing it."

– Greg Anderson

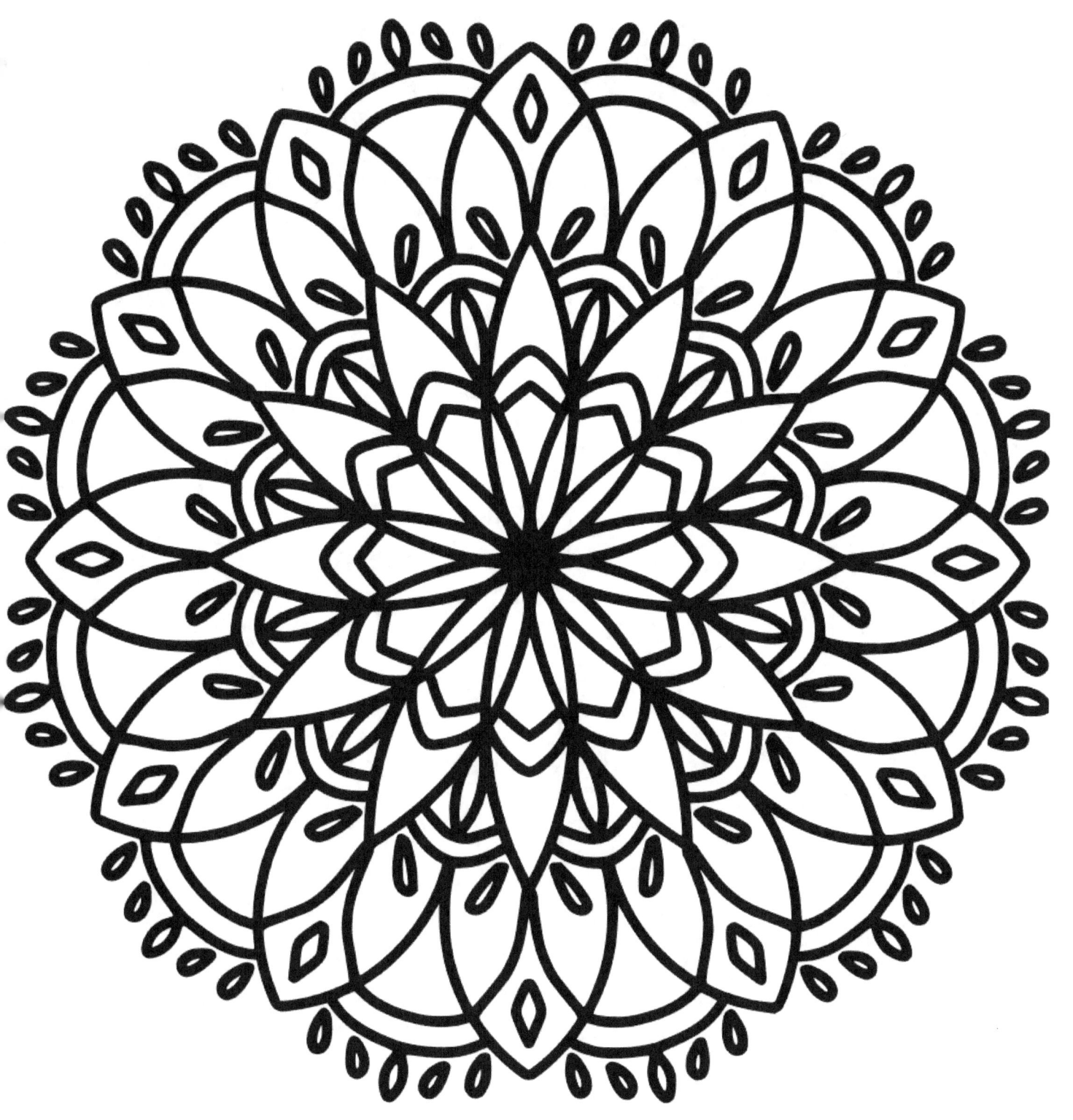

"The happiness of your life depends upon the quality of your thoughts."

-Marcus Aurelius

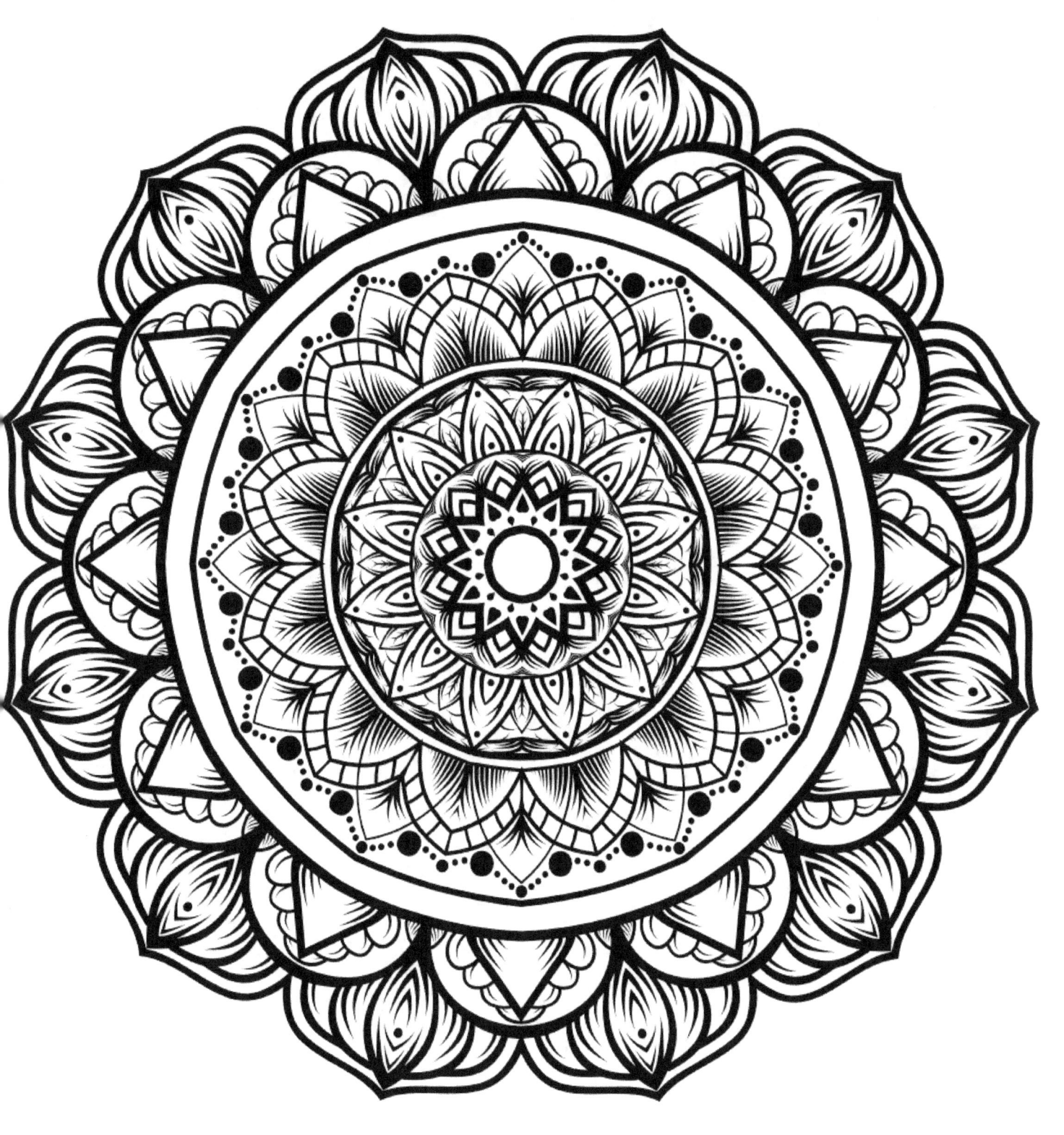

"Self-growth is the driving force behind success and growth."

– Unknown

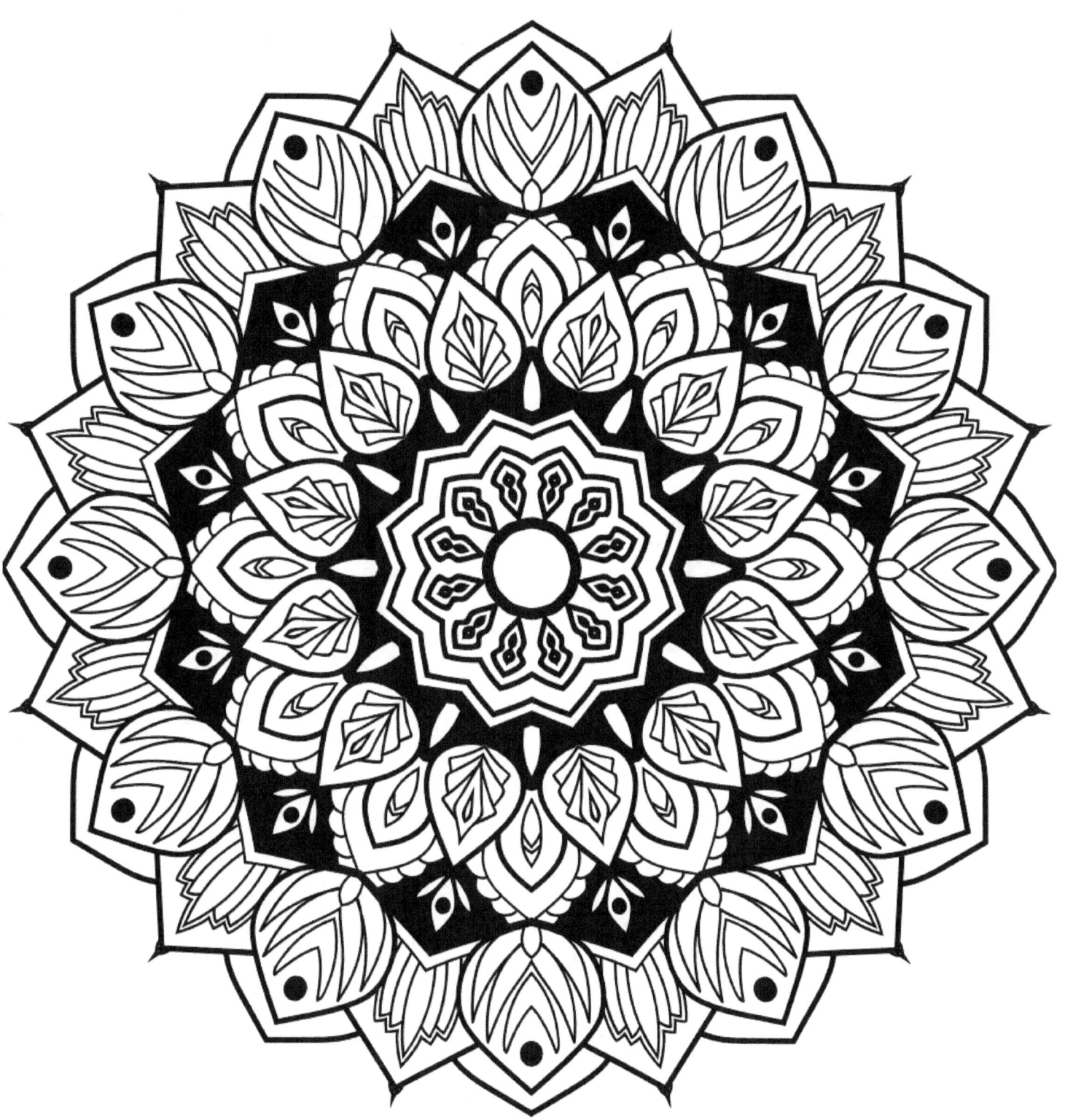

"Life is not measured by the number of breaths we take, but by the moments that take our breath away."

- Unknown

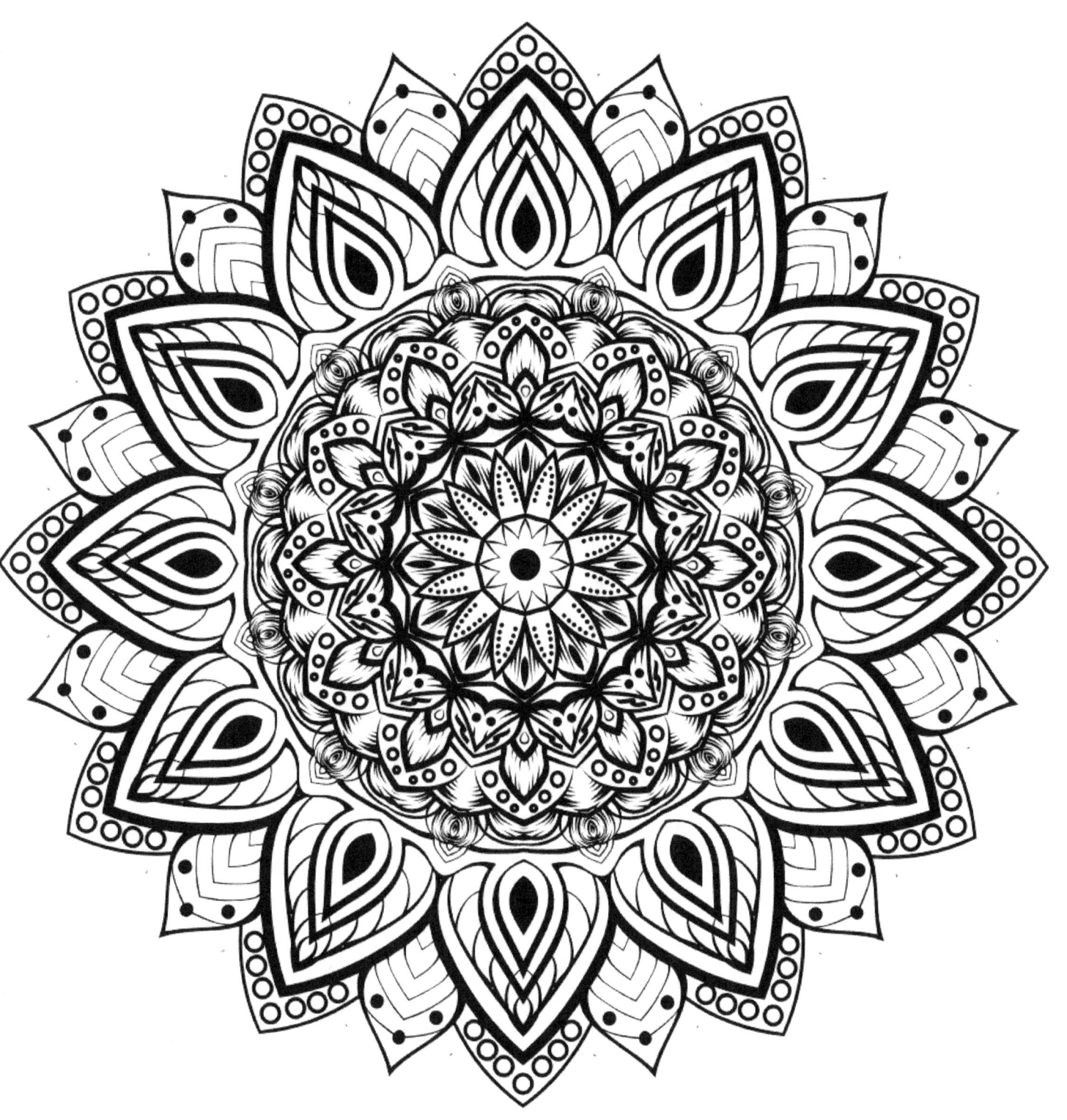

"Life is a collection of moments; cherish the good ones, learn from the tough ones."

– Unknown

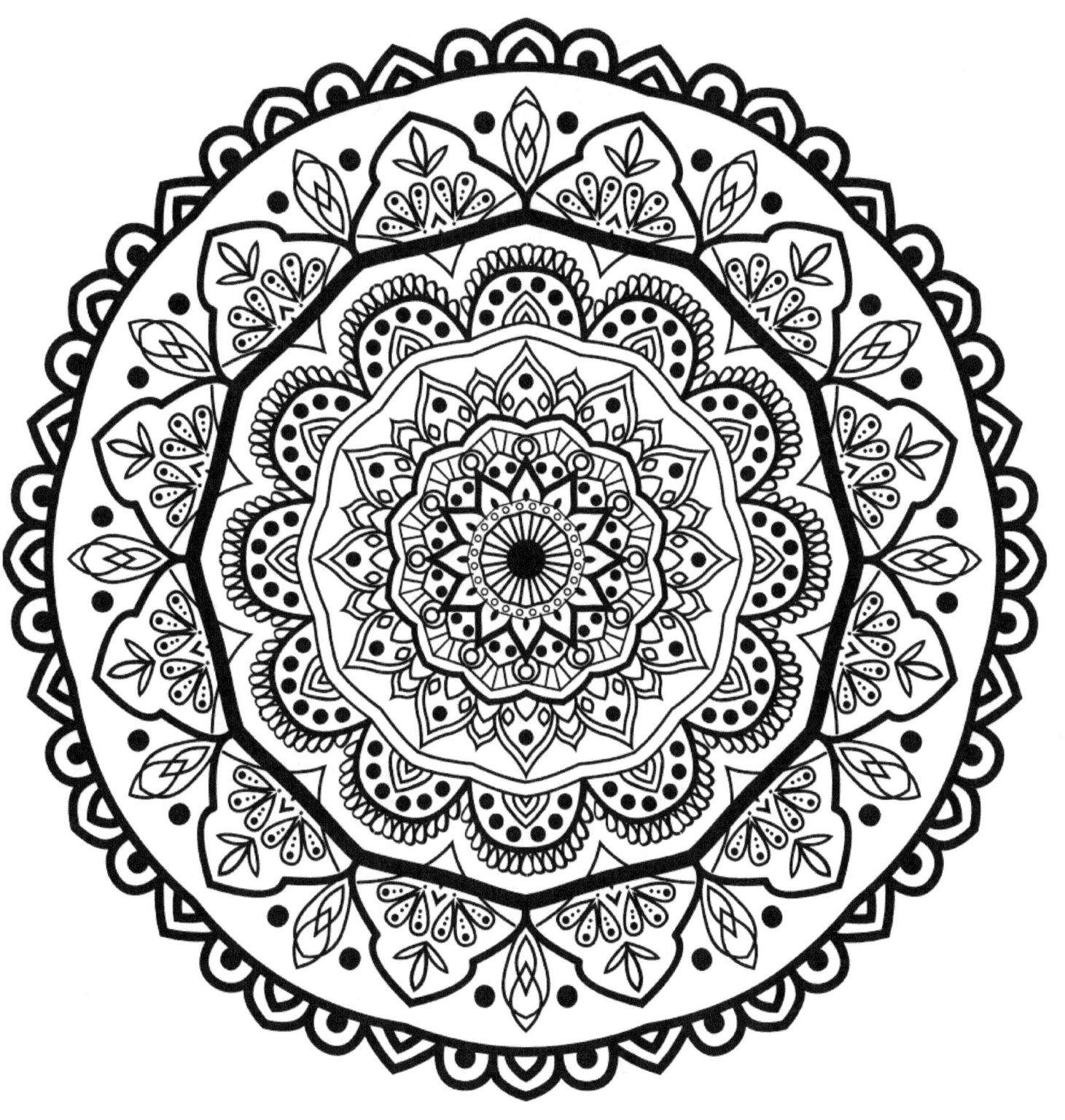

"Life is a journey with problems to solve, lessons to learn, but most importantly, experiences to enjoy."

– Unknown

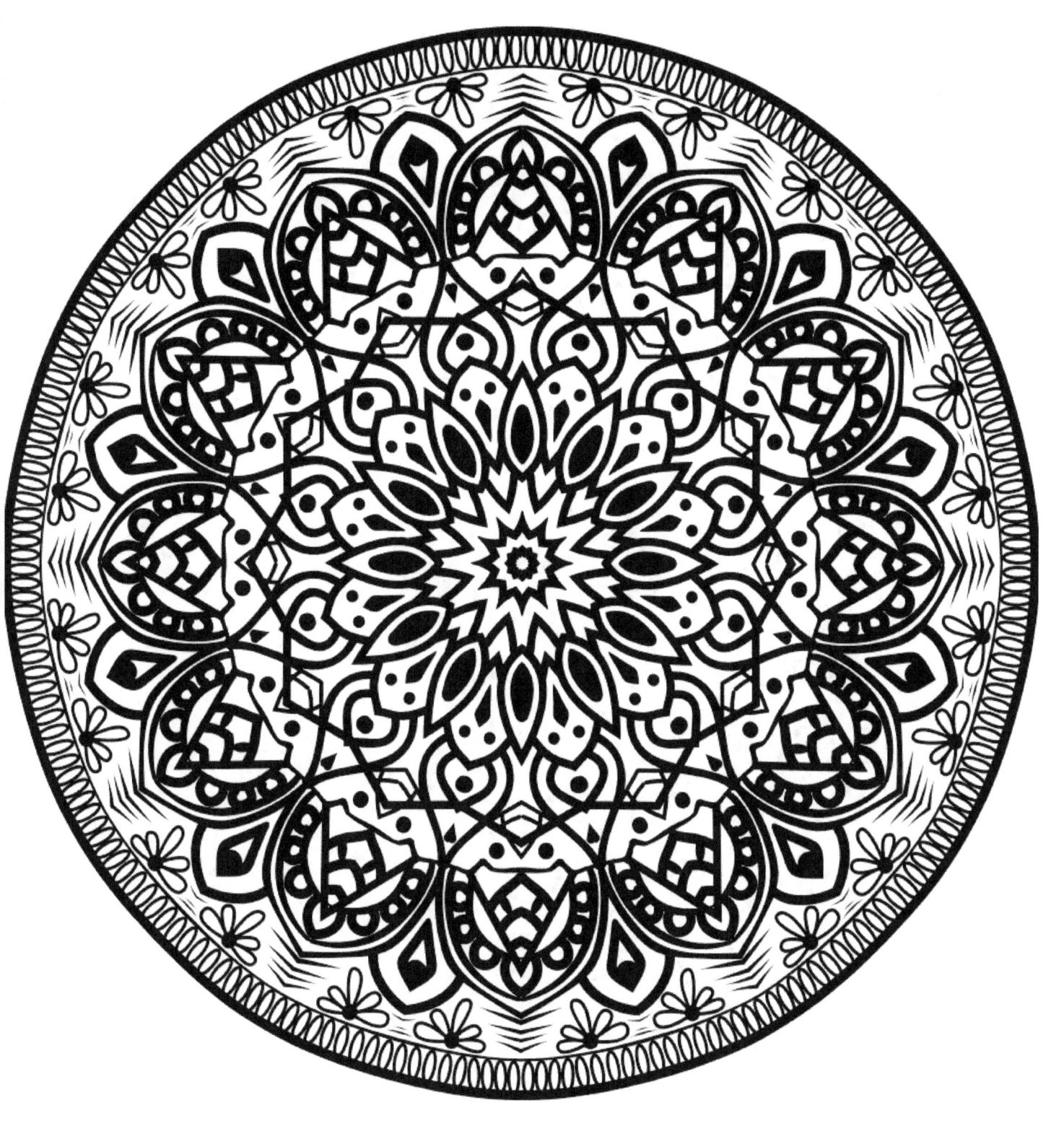

"Life is short, and it's up to you to make it sweet."

-Sarah L. Delany

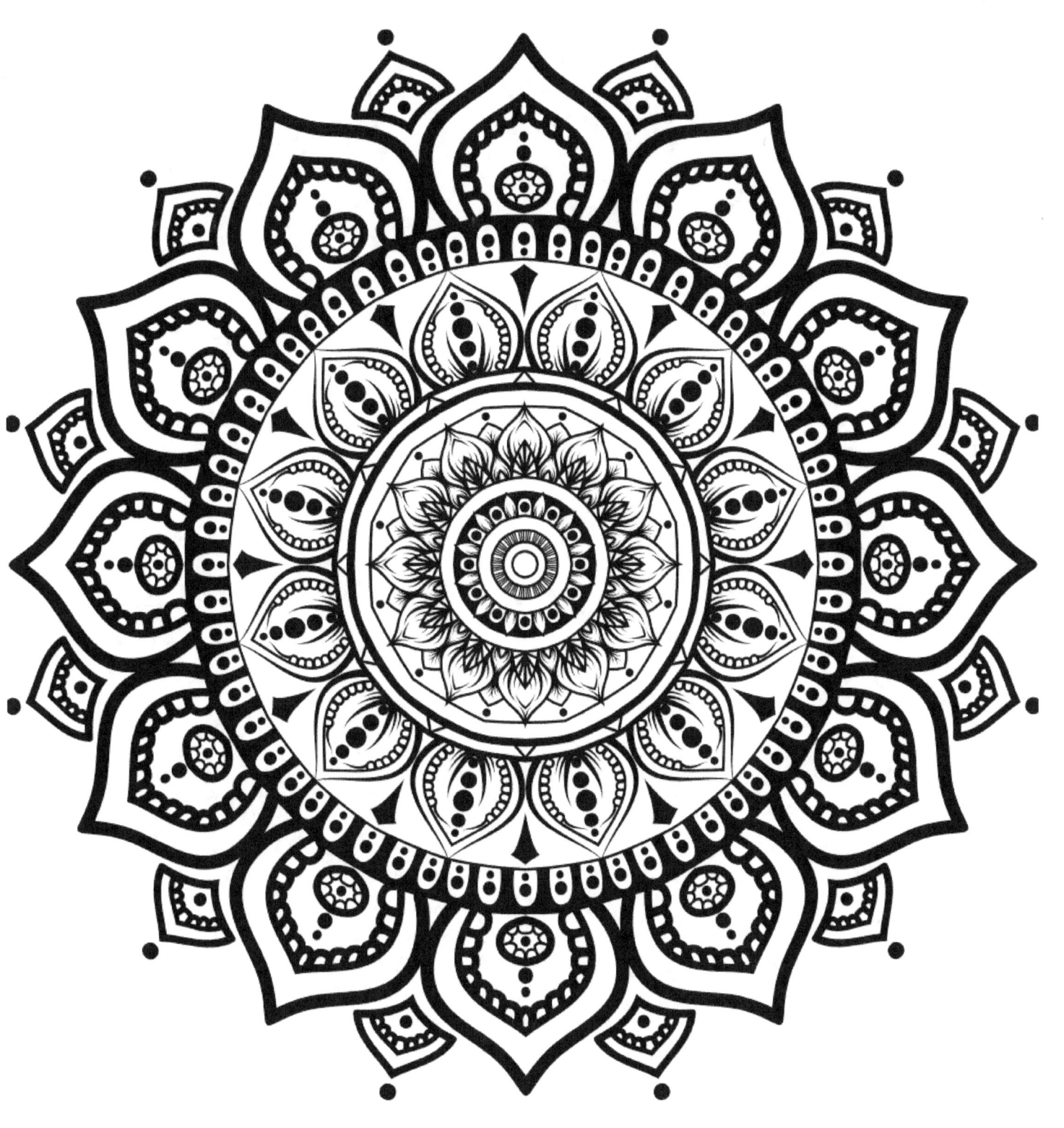

"Believe you can and you're halfway there."

- Theodore Roosevelt

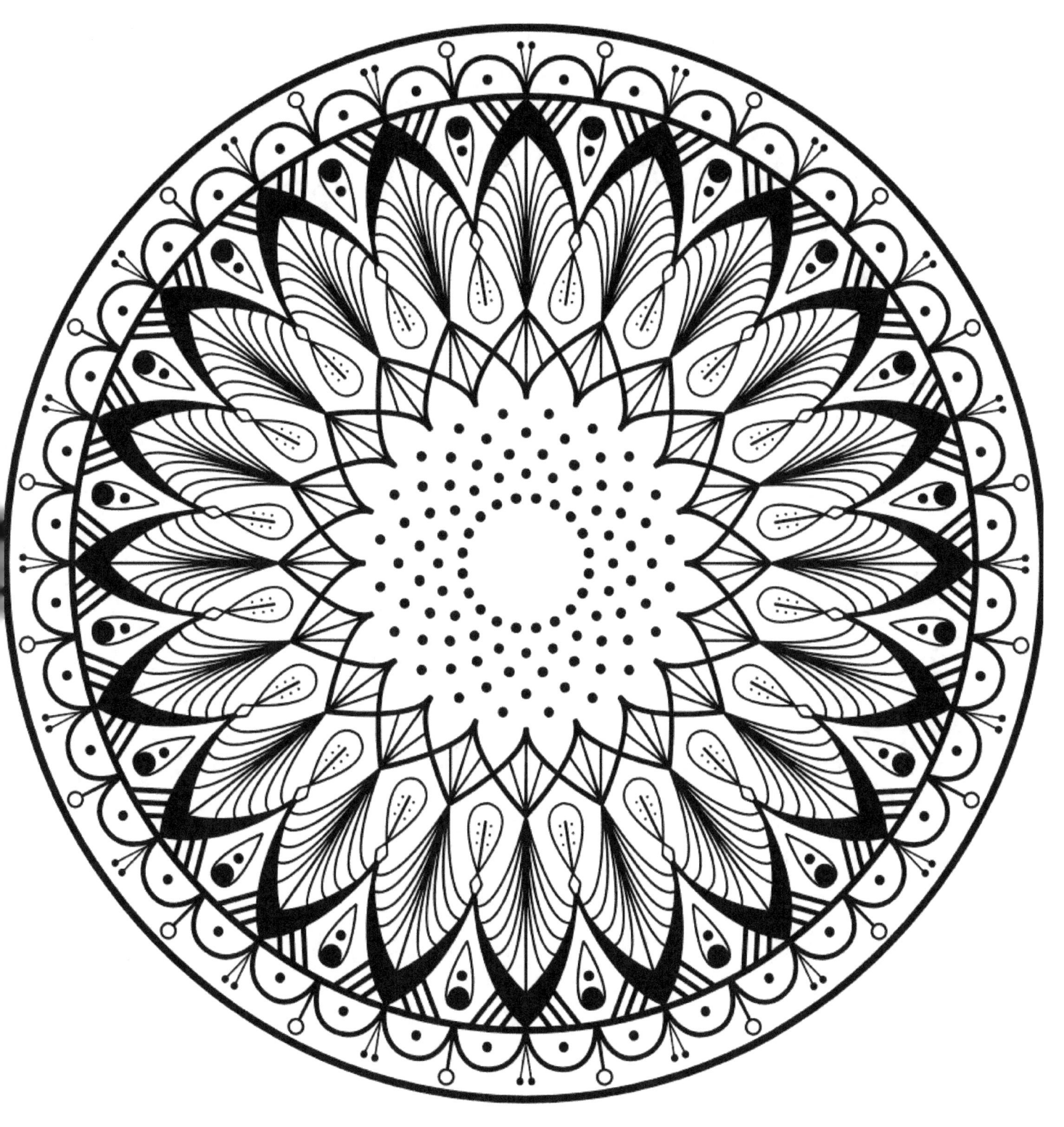

"Life is not about waiting for the storm to pass but learning to dance in the rain."

- Vivian Greene

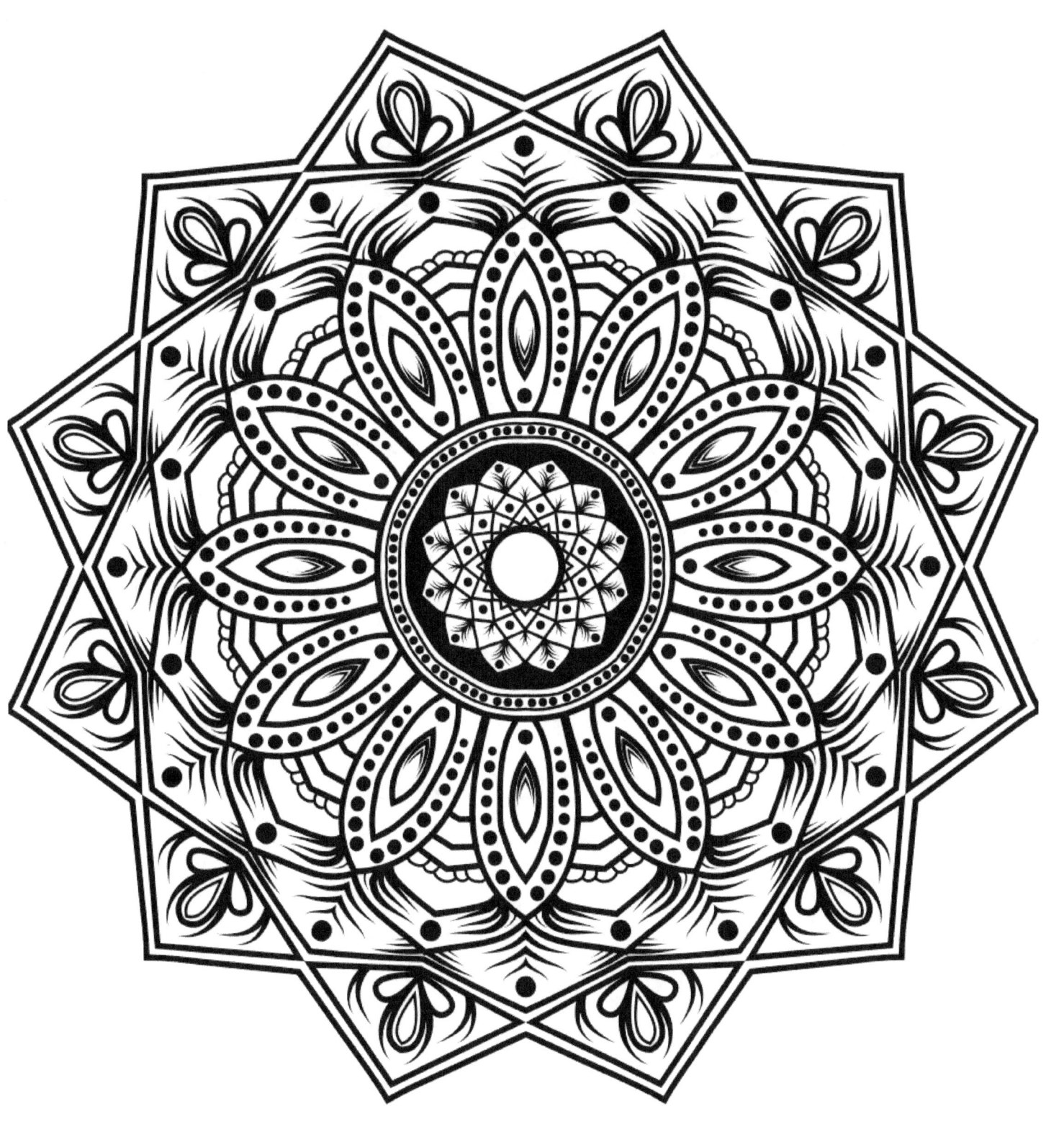

"The only limit to our realization of tomorrow will be our doubts of today."

- Franklin D. Roosevelt

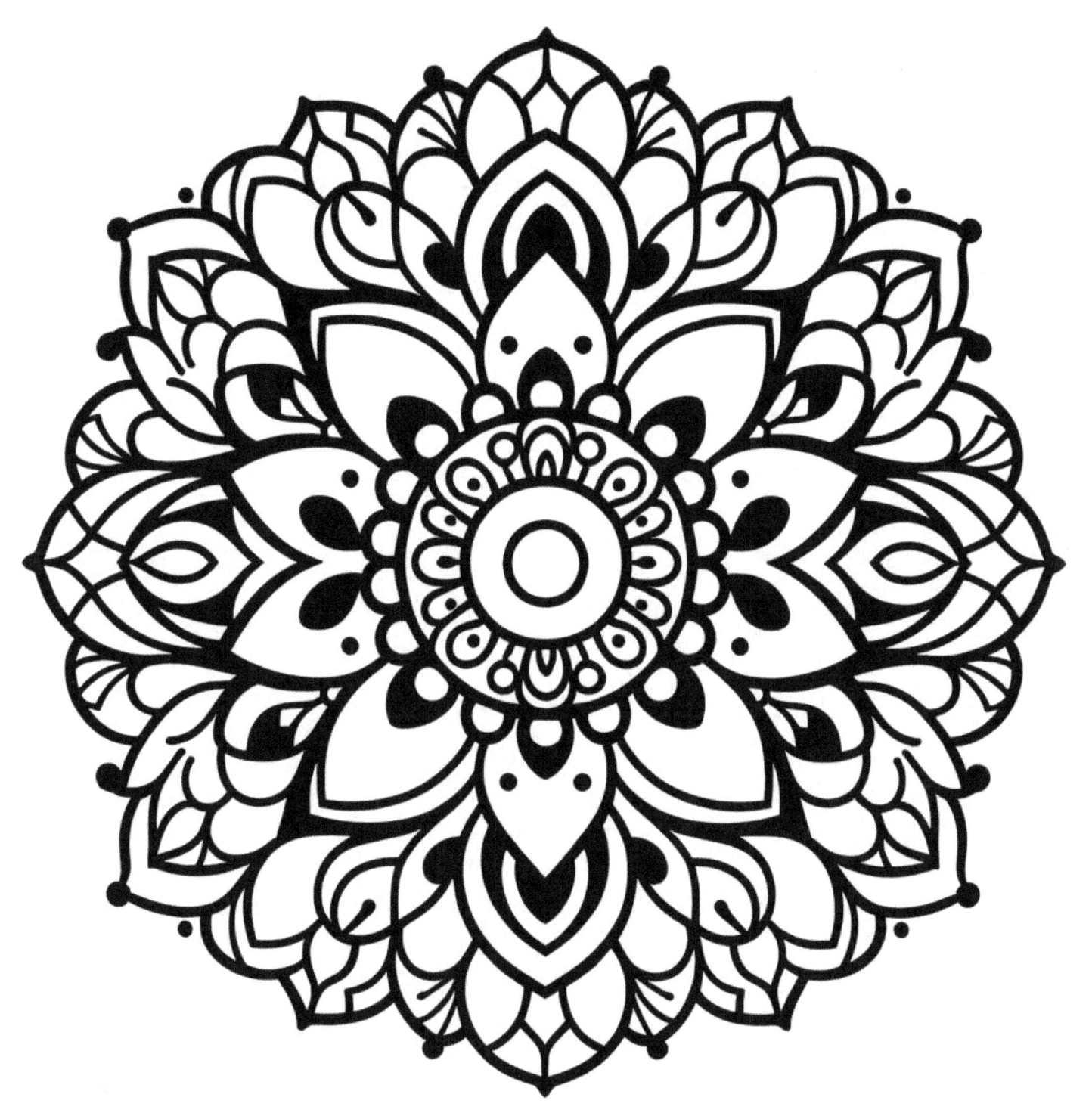

"Success is not final, failure is not fatal: It is the courage to continue that counts."

- Winston Churchill

"The only way to do great work is to love what you do."

- Steve Jobs

"Difficult roads often lead to beautiful destinations."

- Zig Ziglar

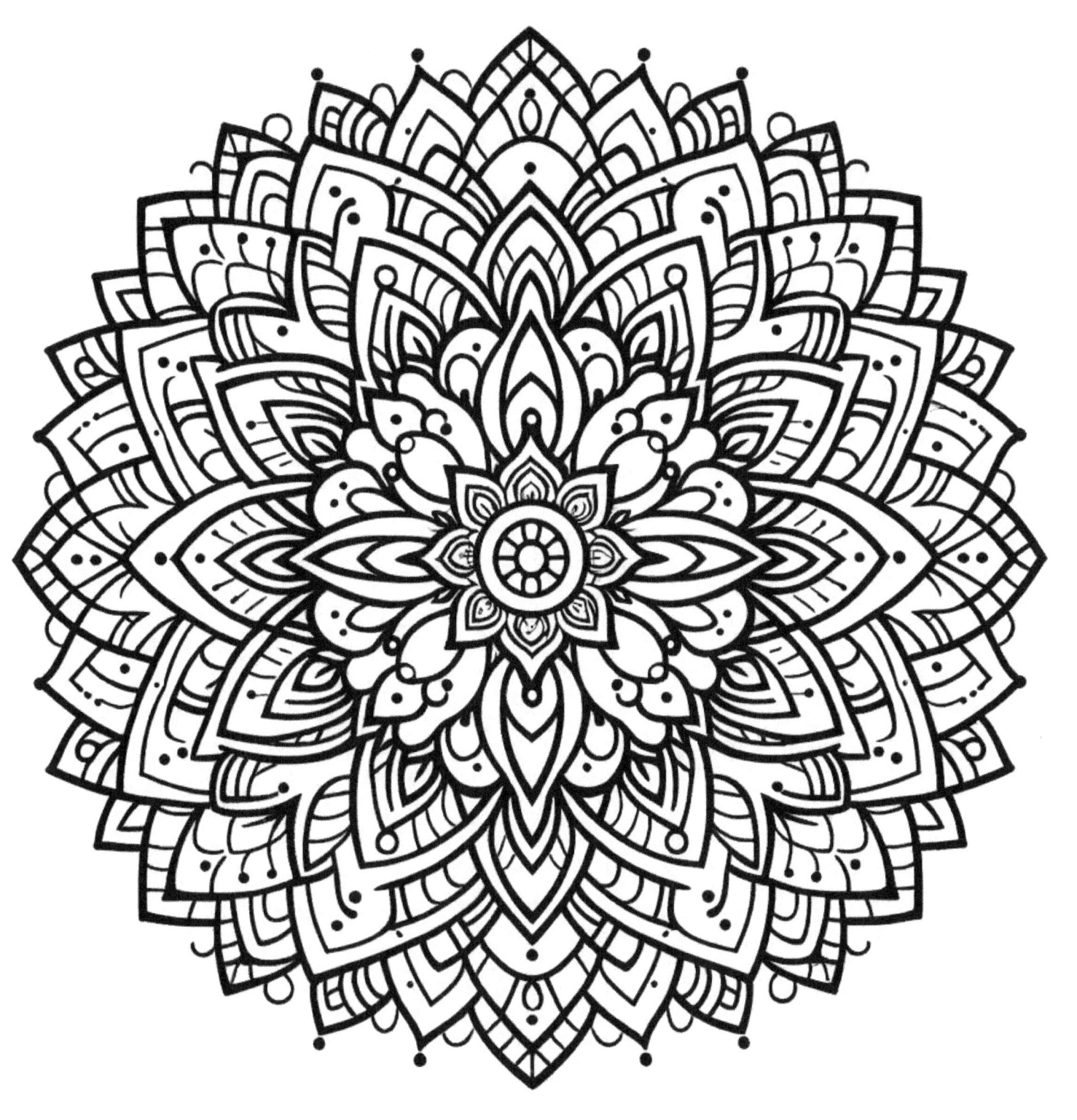

"The secret of getting ahead is getting started."

- Mark Twain

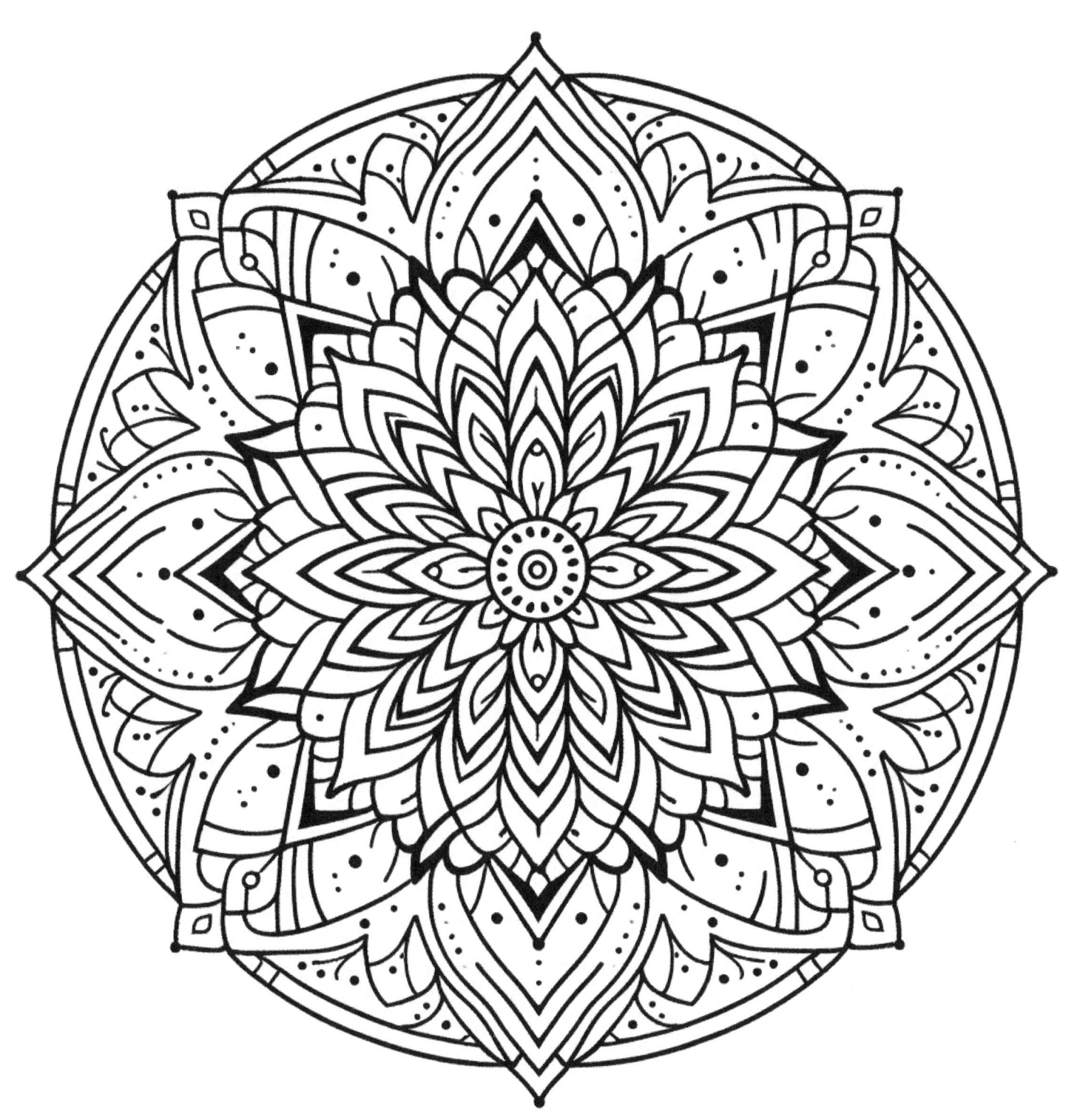

"You are braver than you believe, stronger than you seem, and smarter than you think."

- A.A. Milne

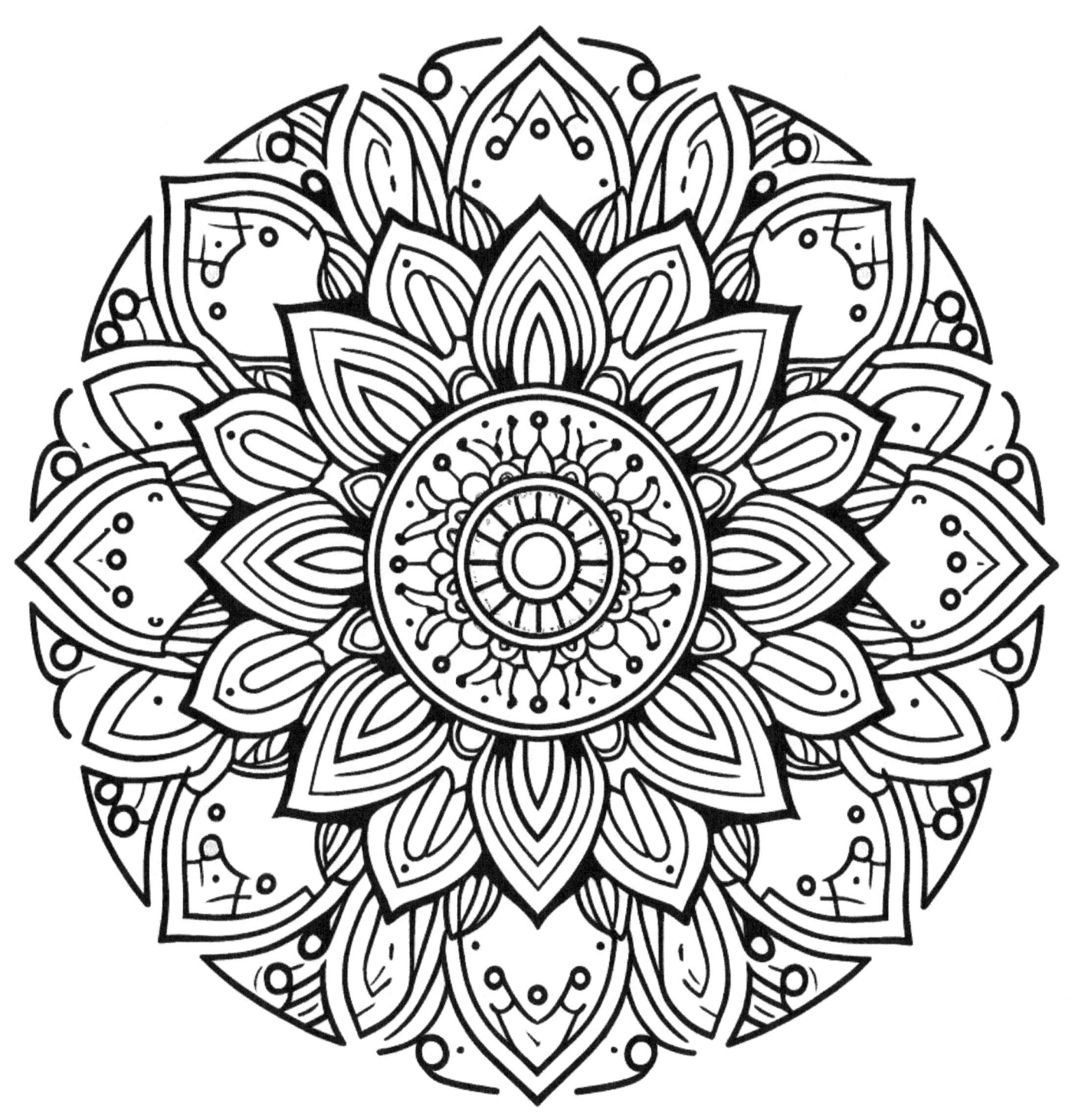

"Optimism is the faith that leads to achievement. Nothing can be done without hope and confidence."

- Helen Keller

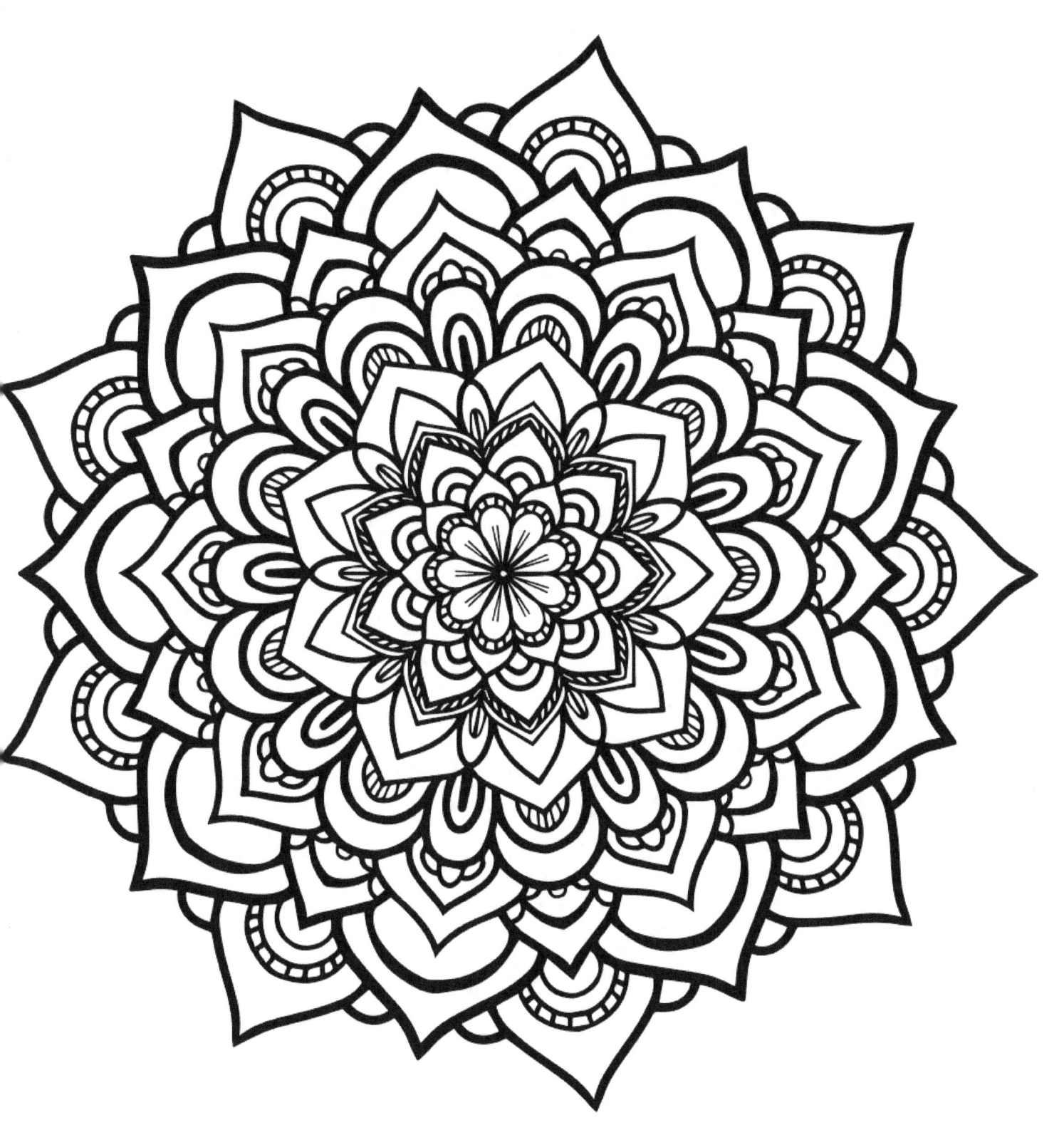

"The future belongs to those who believe in the beauty of their dreams."

- Eleanor Roosevelt

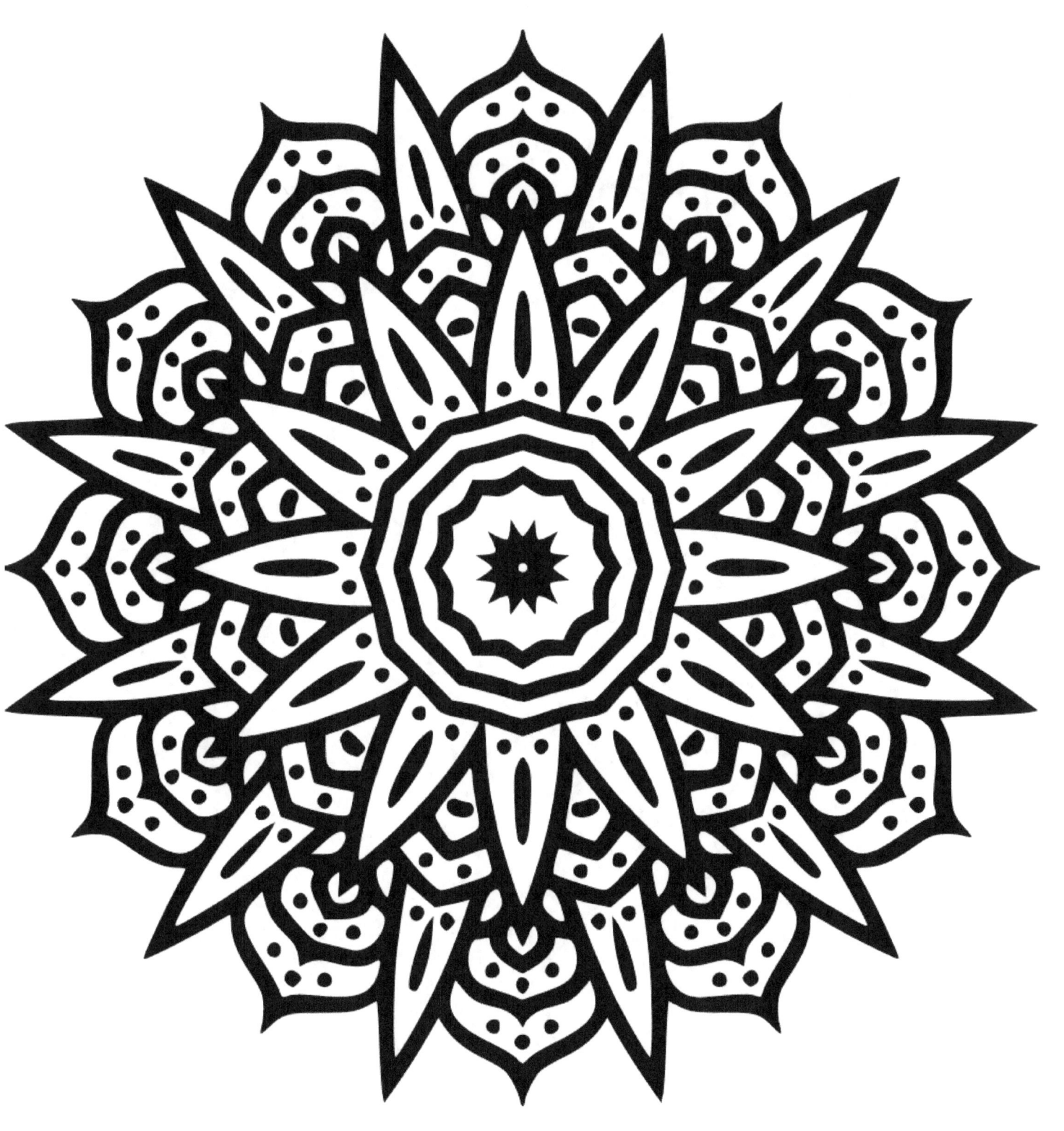

"Life is like riding a bicycle. To keep your balance, you must keep moving."

- Albert Einstein

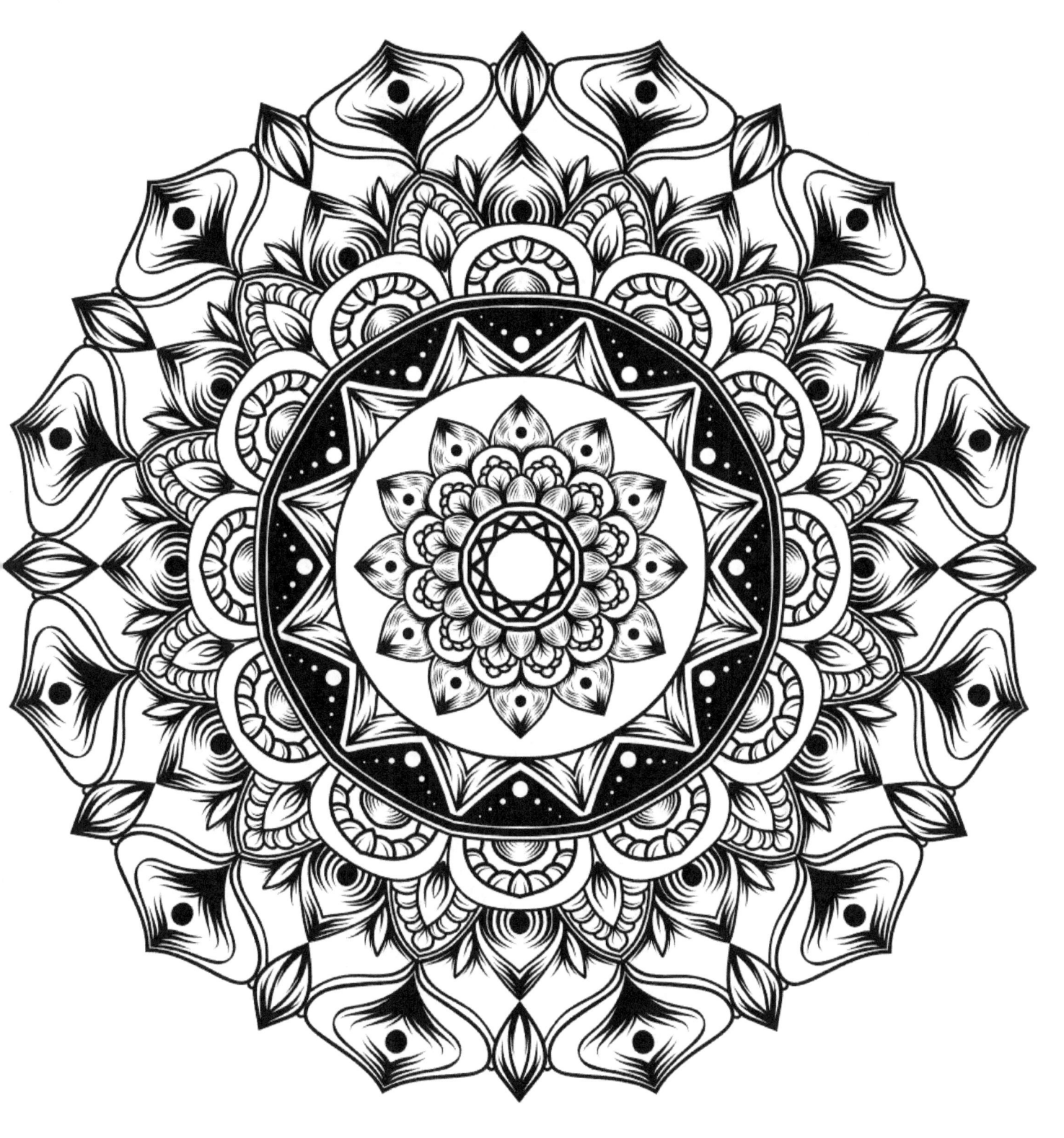

"Happiness is not by chance, but by choice."

- Jim Rohn

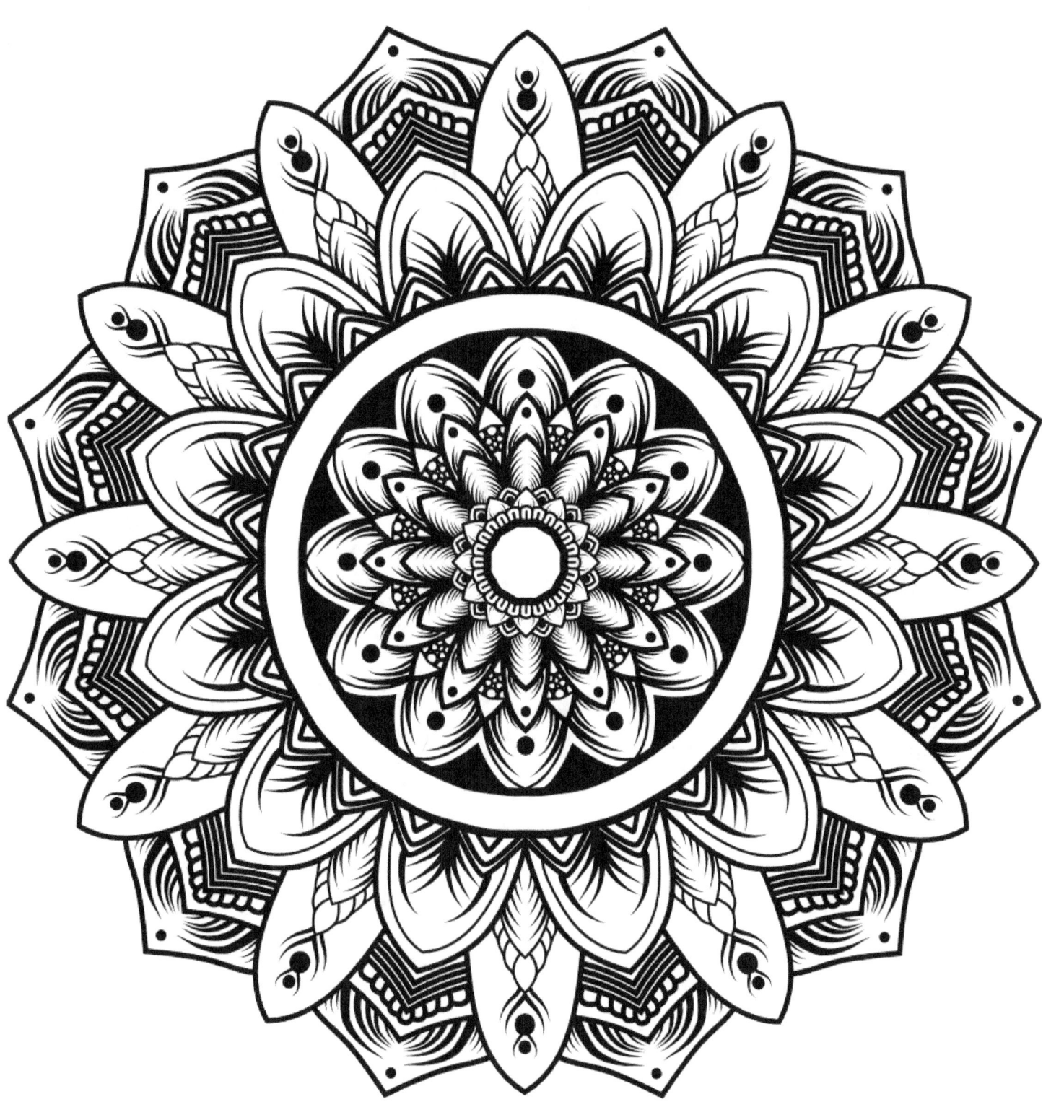

"The greatest glory in living lies not in never falling, but in rising every time we fall."

- Ralph Waldo Emerson

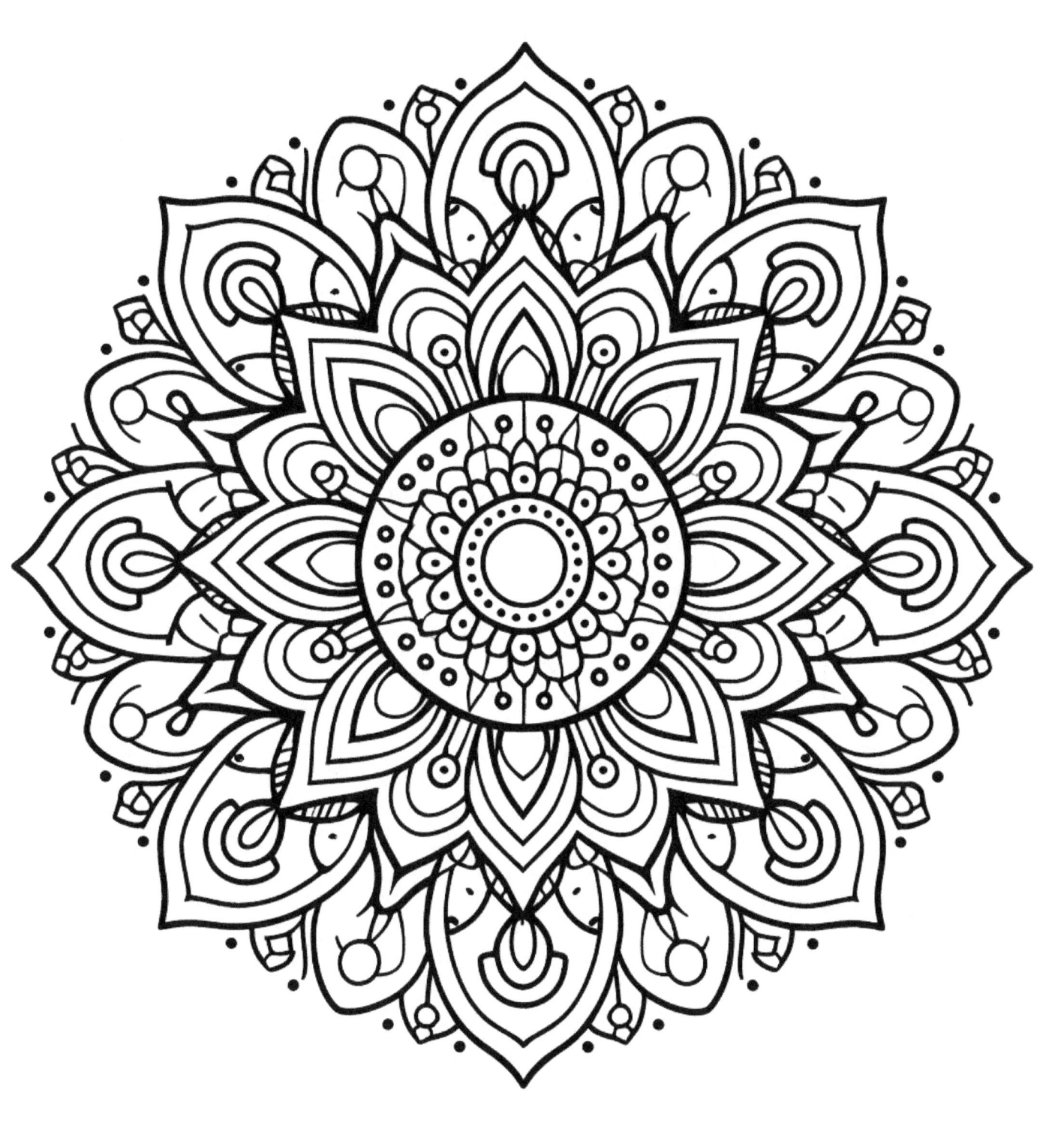

"Be yourself; everyone else is already taken."

– Oscar Wilde

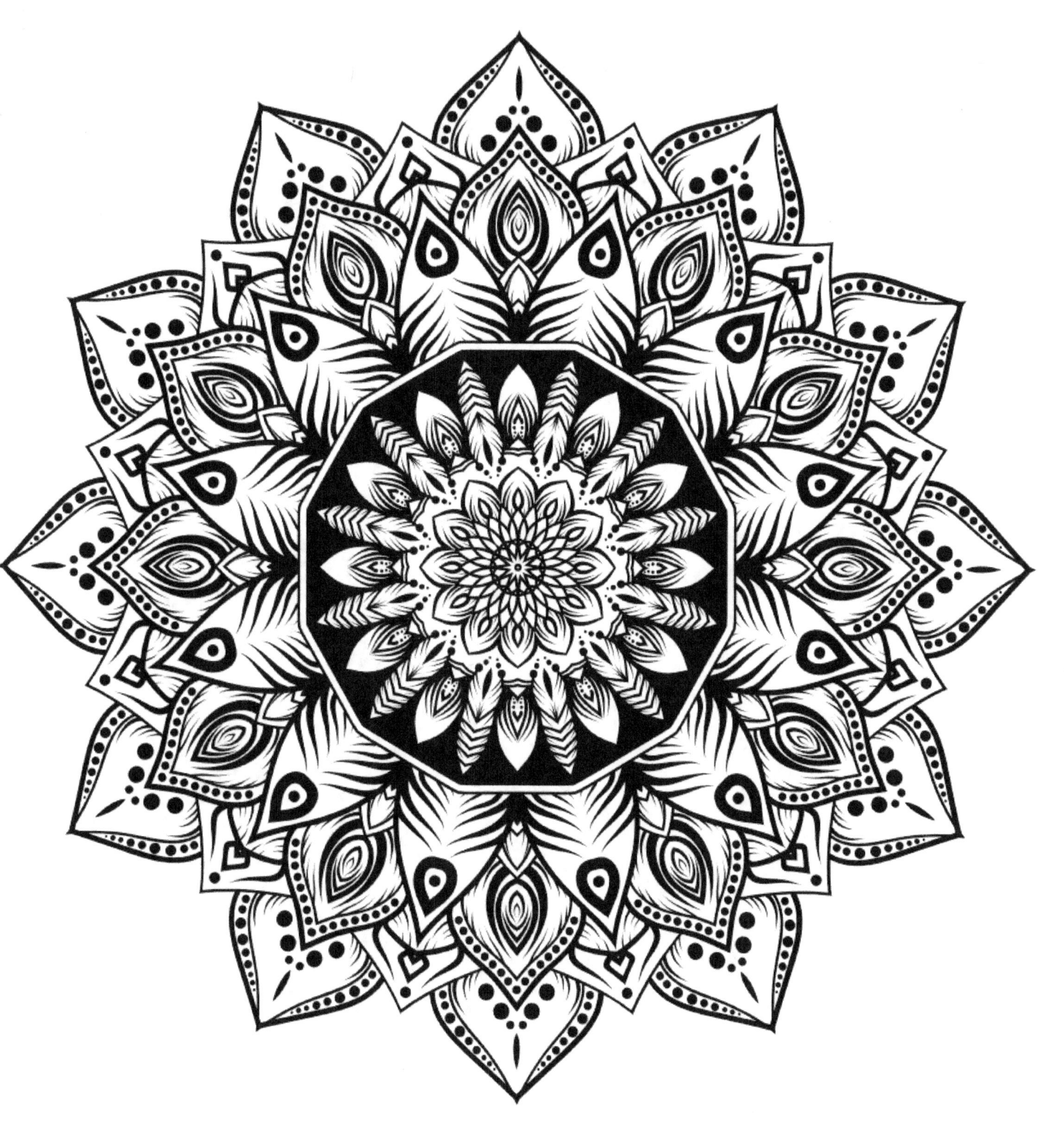

"You miss 100% of the shots you don't take."

- Wayne Gretzky

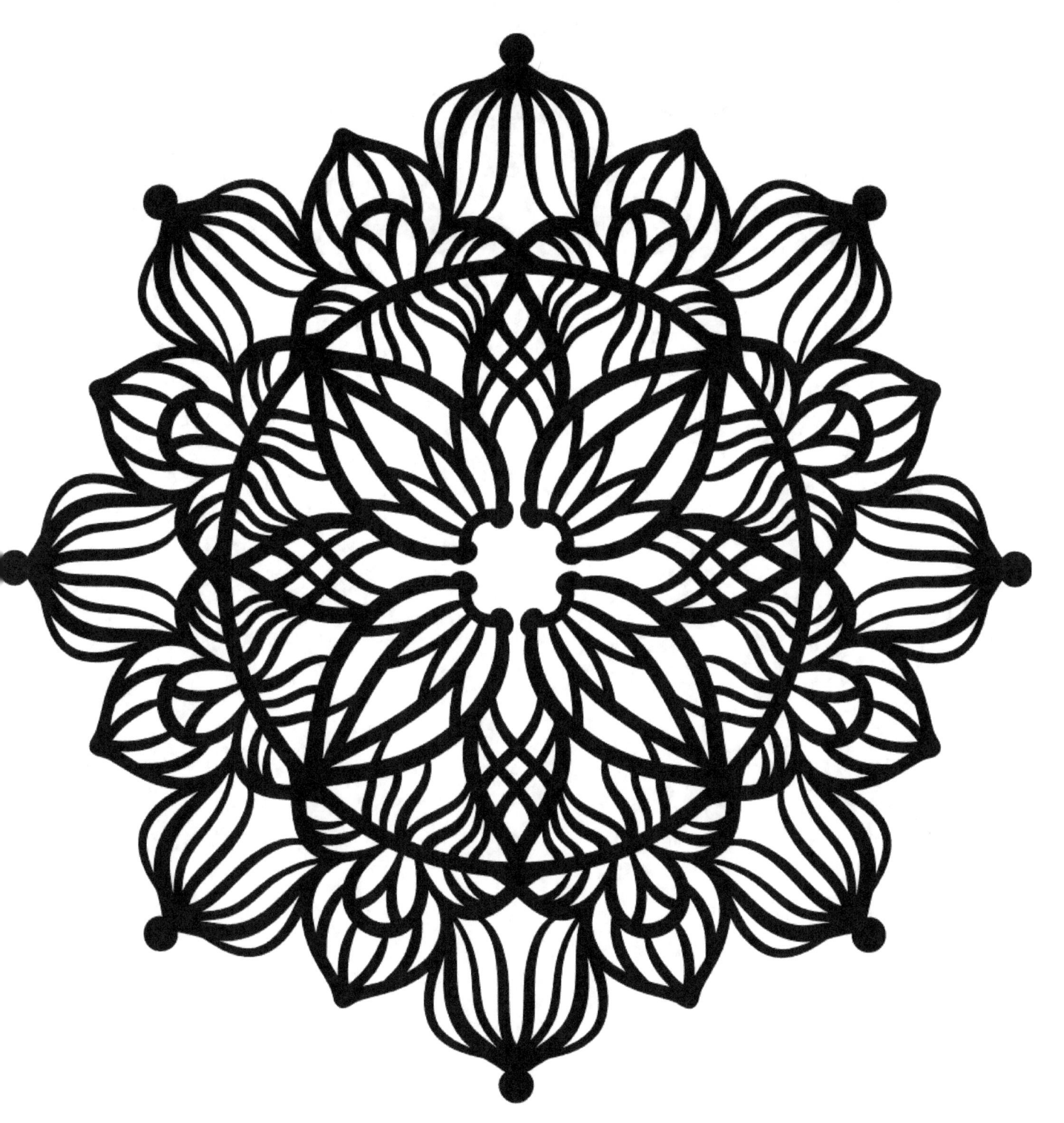

"Success is not the key to happiness. Happiness is the key to success. If you love what you are doing, you will be successful."

- Albert Schweitzer

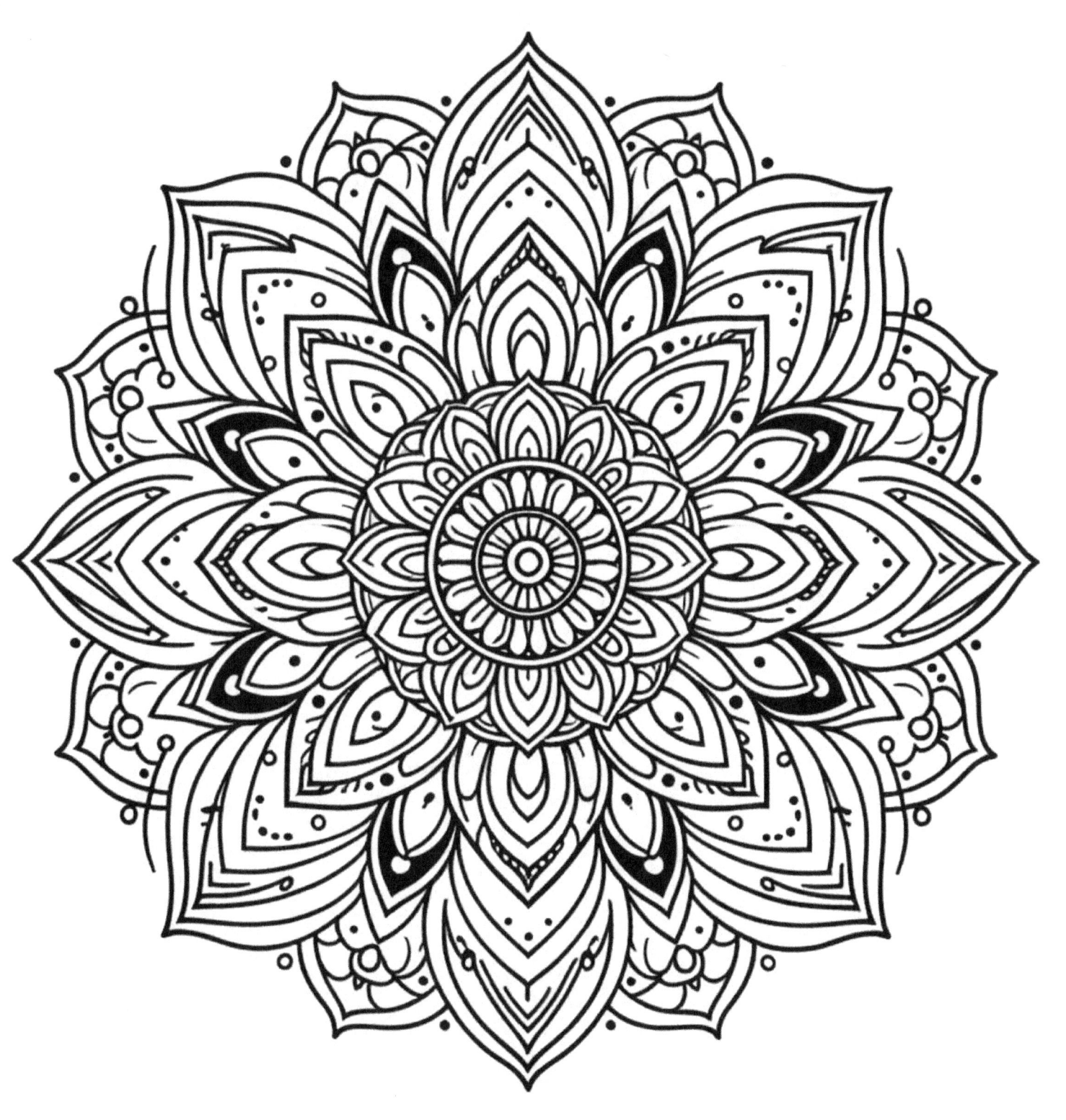

"The key to keeping your balance is knowing when you've lost it."

- Unknown

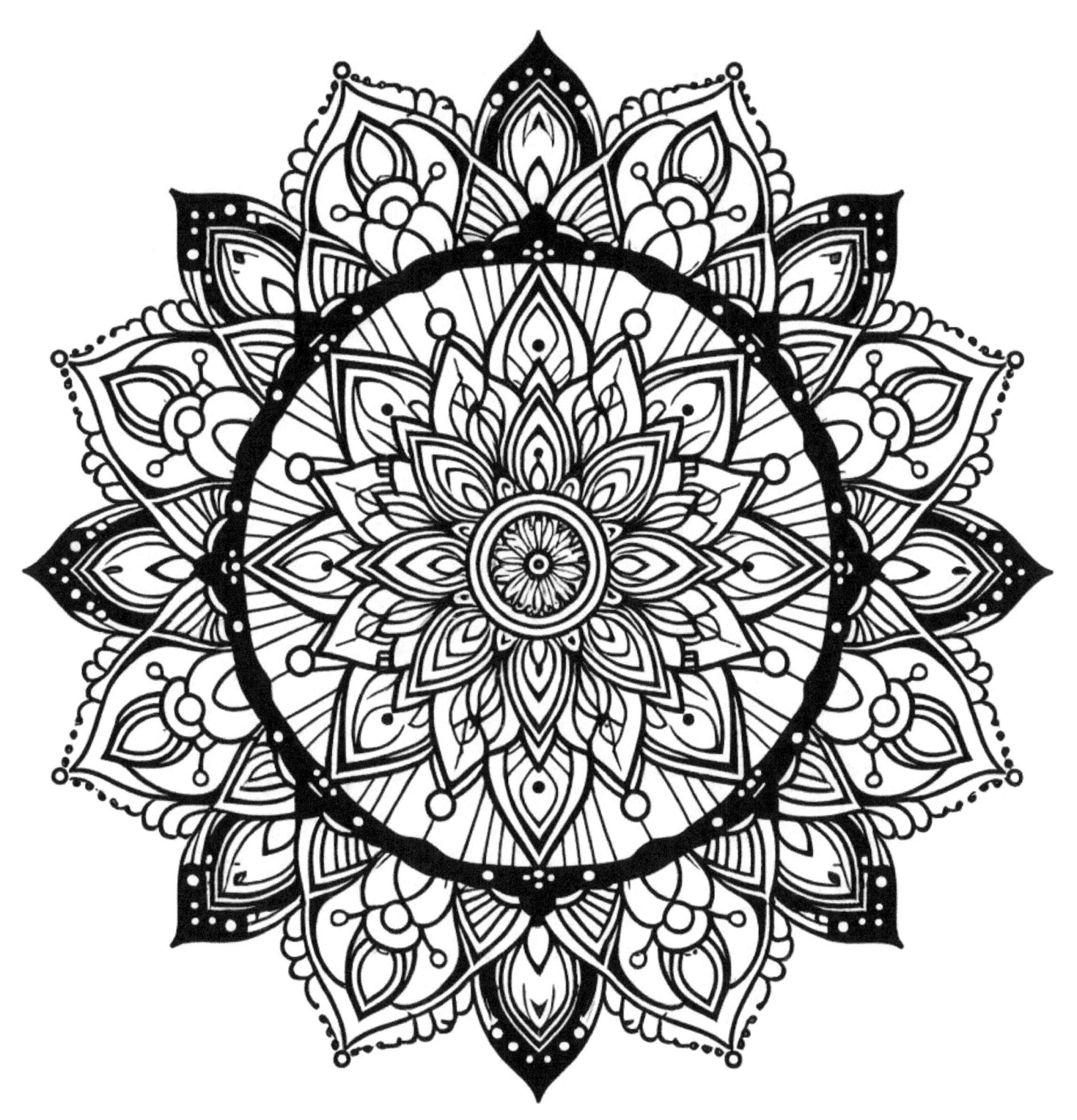

"It's not the years in your life that count. It's the life in your years."

– Abraham Lincoln

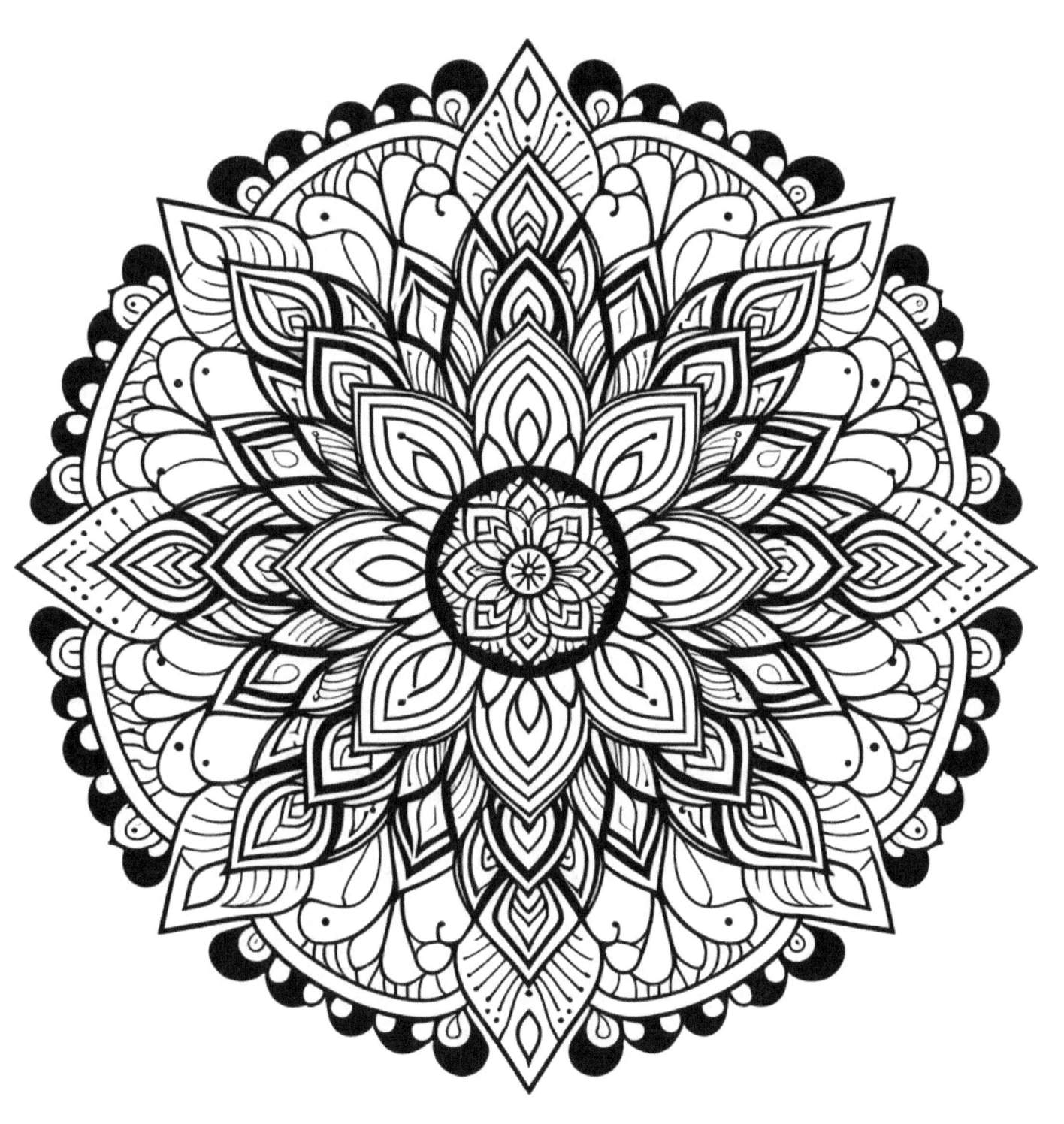

"Don't count the days, make the days count."

- Muhammad Ali

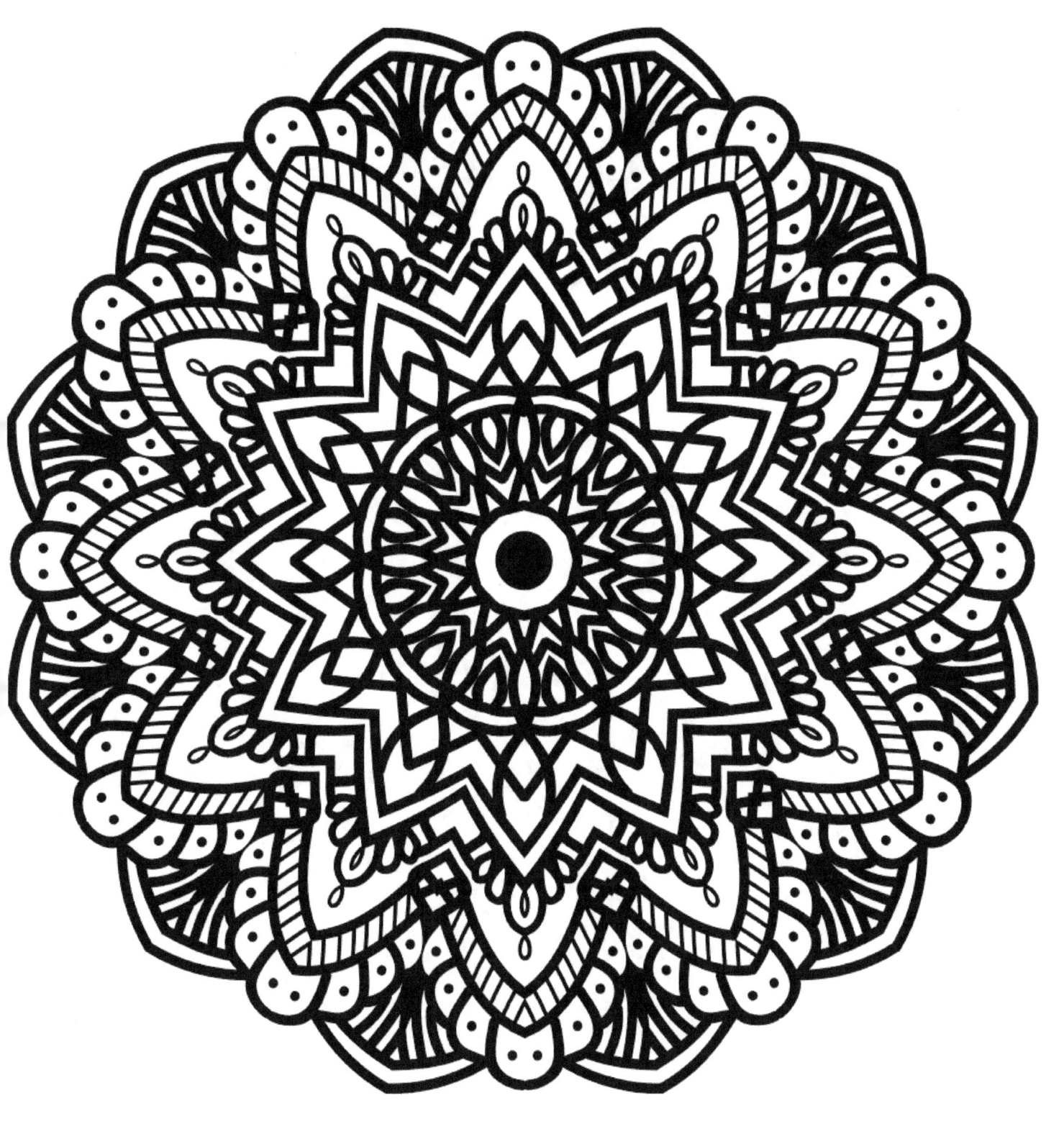

"The journey of a thousand miles begins with a single step."

- Lau Tzu

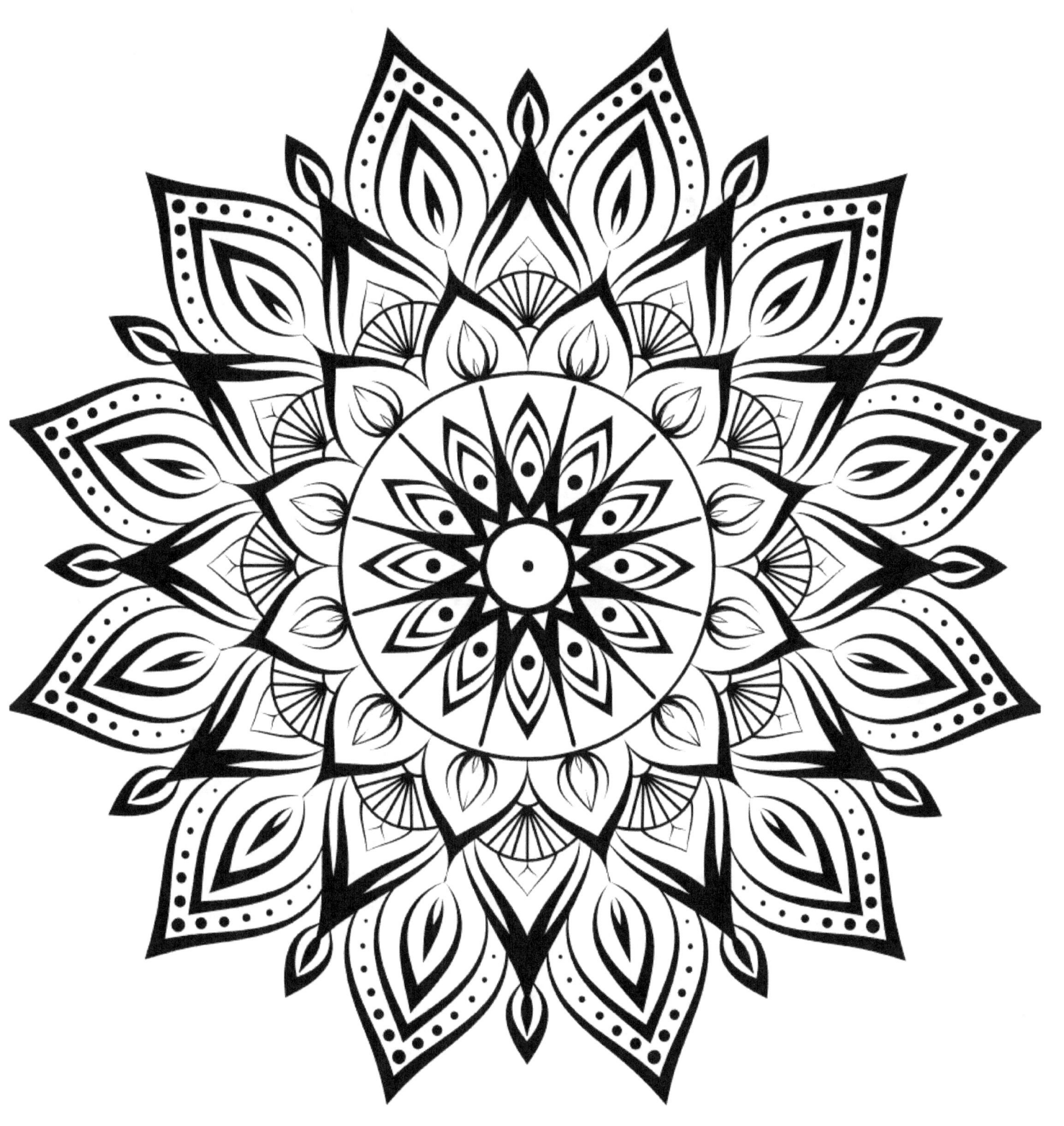

"Life is a canvas; paint it with the colours of gratitude and kindness."

- Unknown

Life is a canvas, and you are the masterpiece.

- Unknown

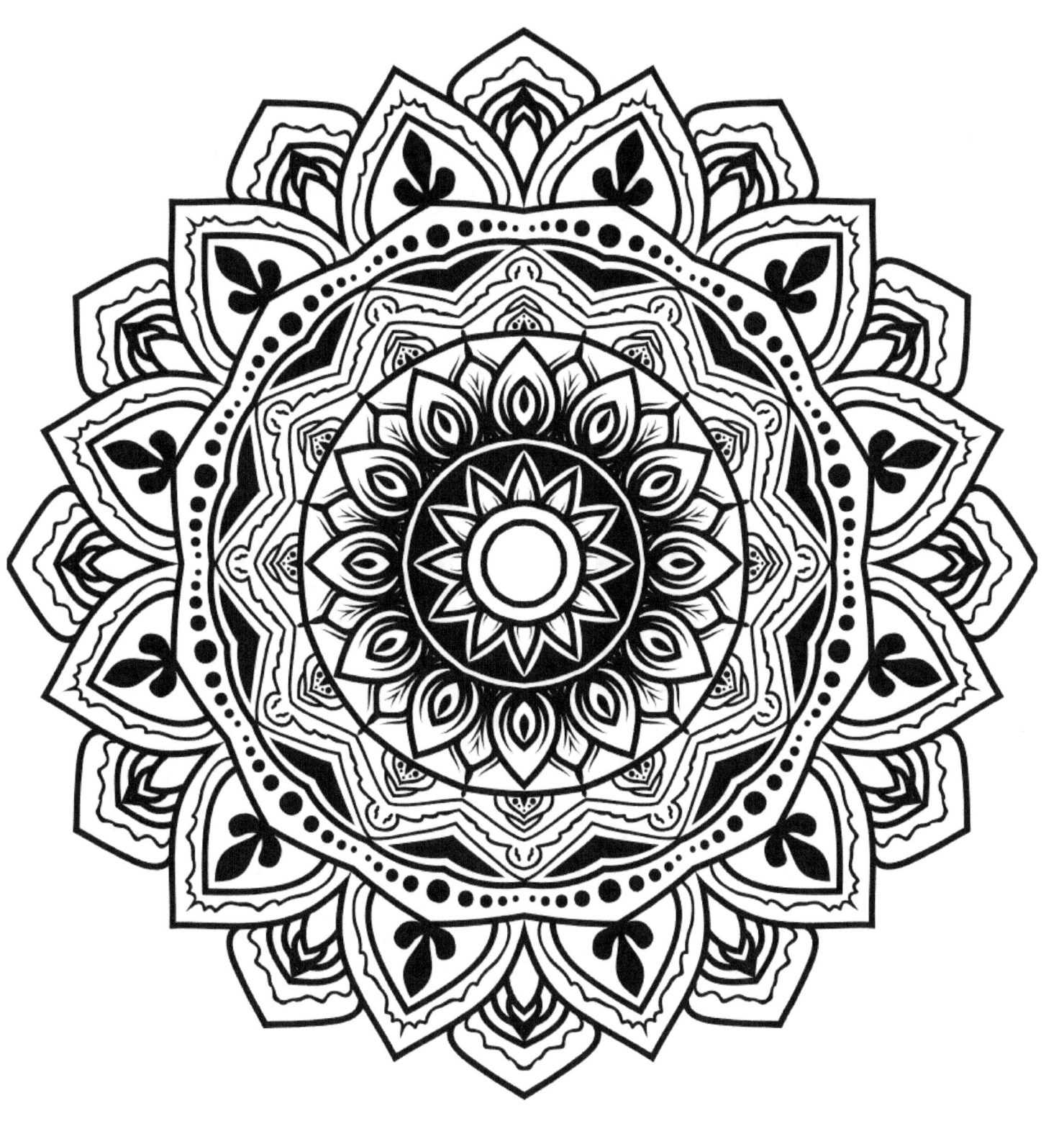

"Like a candle, radiate light even in the darkest of times."

- Unknown

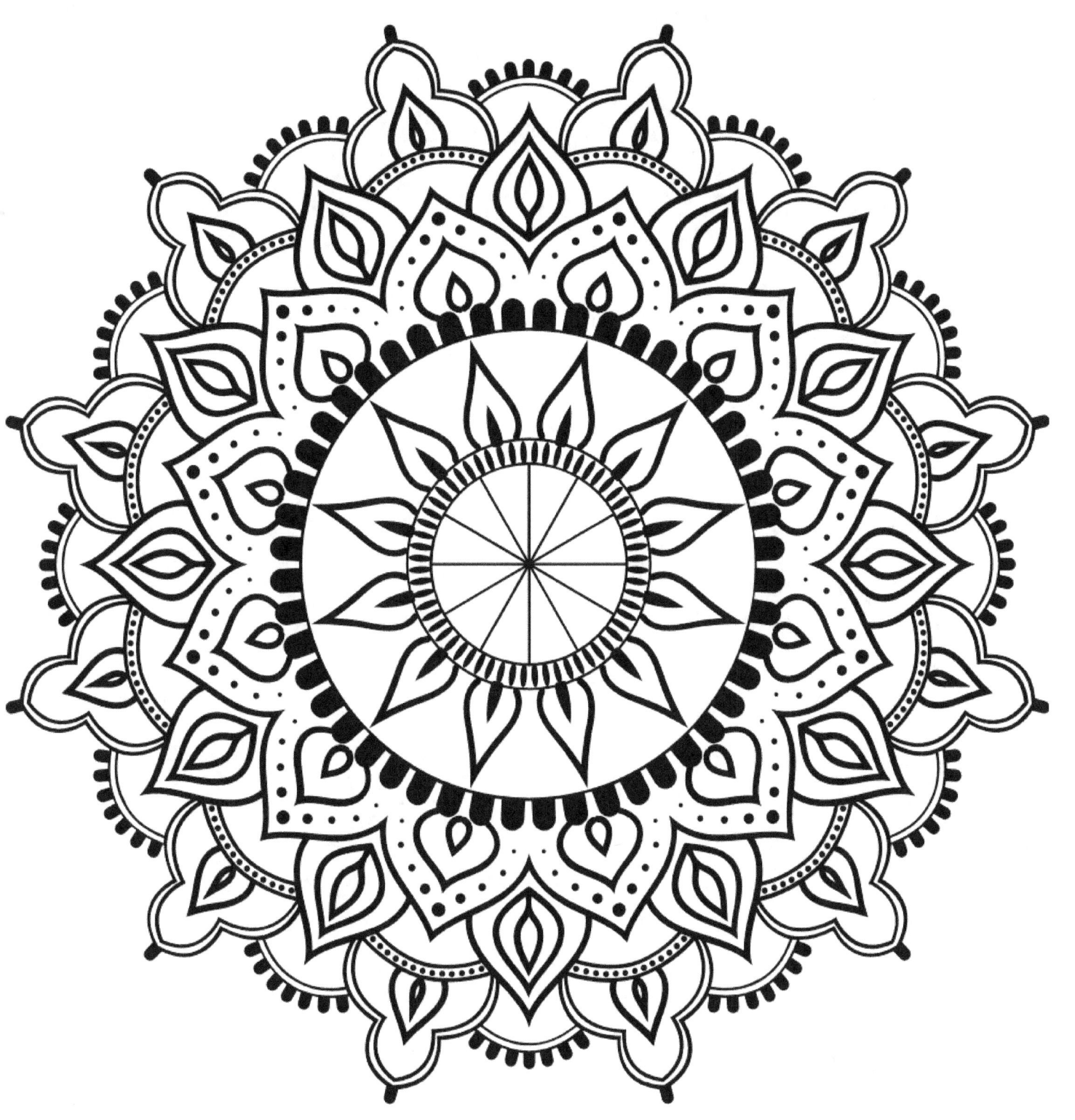

"Embrace the rhythm of your heartbeat and dance to the melody of your soul."

- Unknown

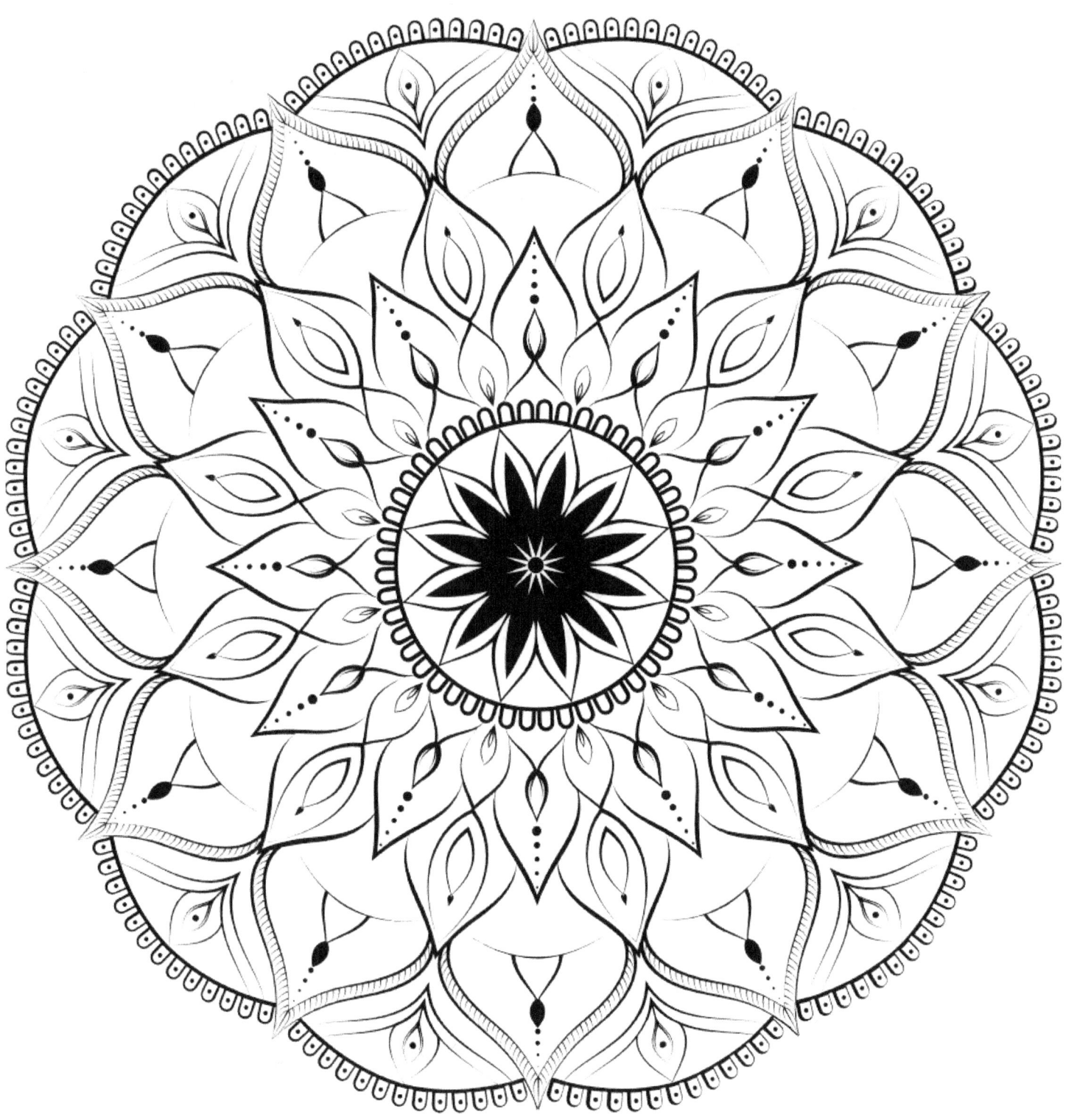

"Let your smile be your compass, guiding you through life's twists and turns."

- Unknown

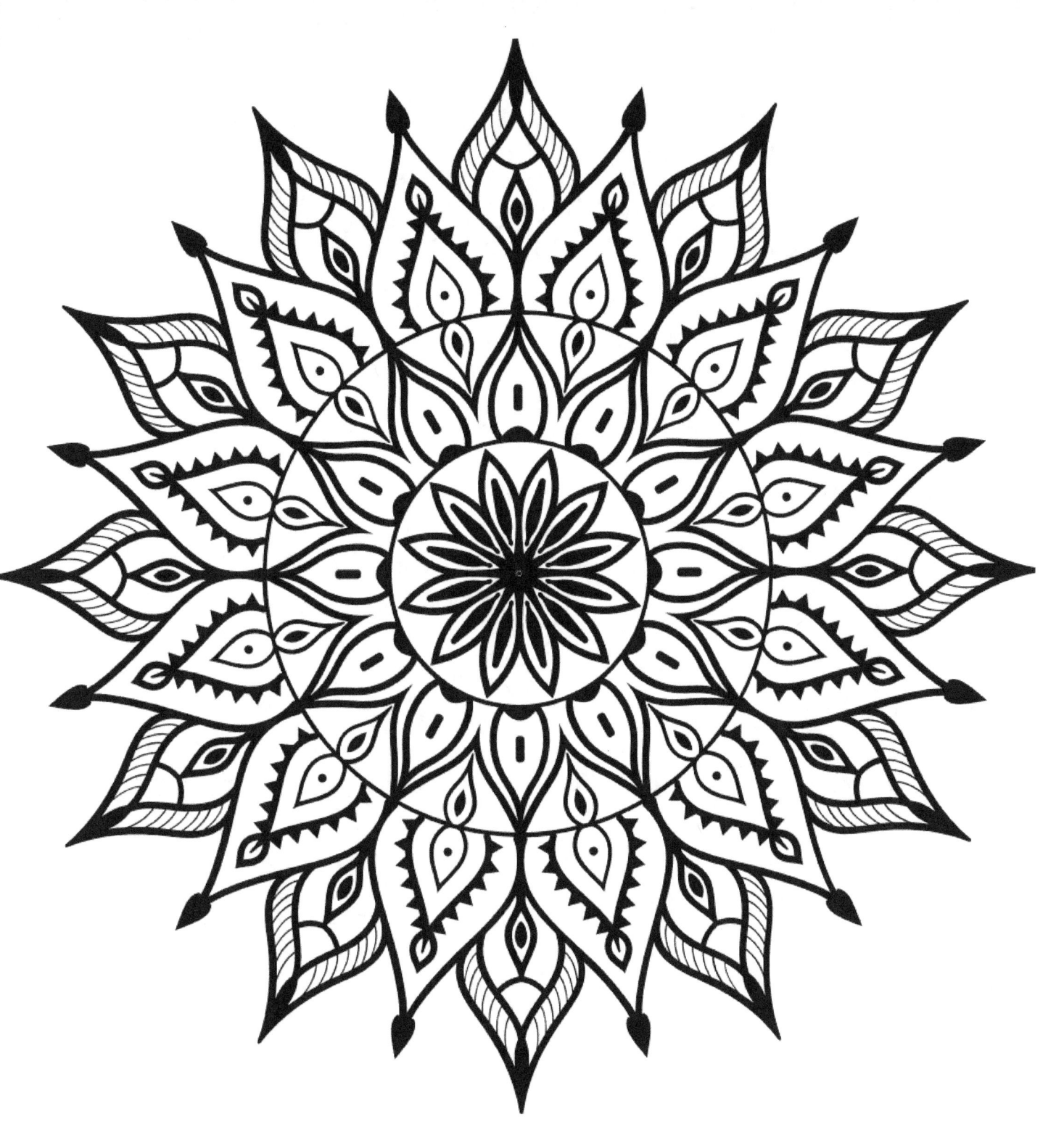

"Sow seeds of positivity and watch them blossom into a garden of possibilities."

– Unknown

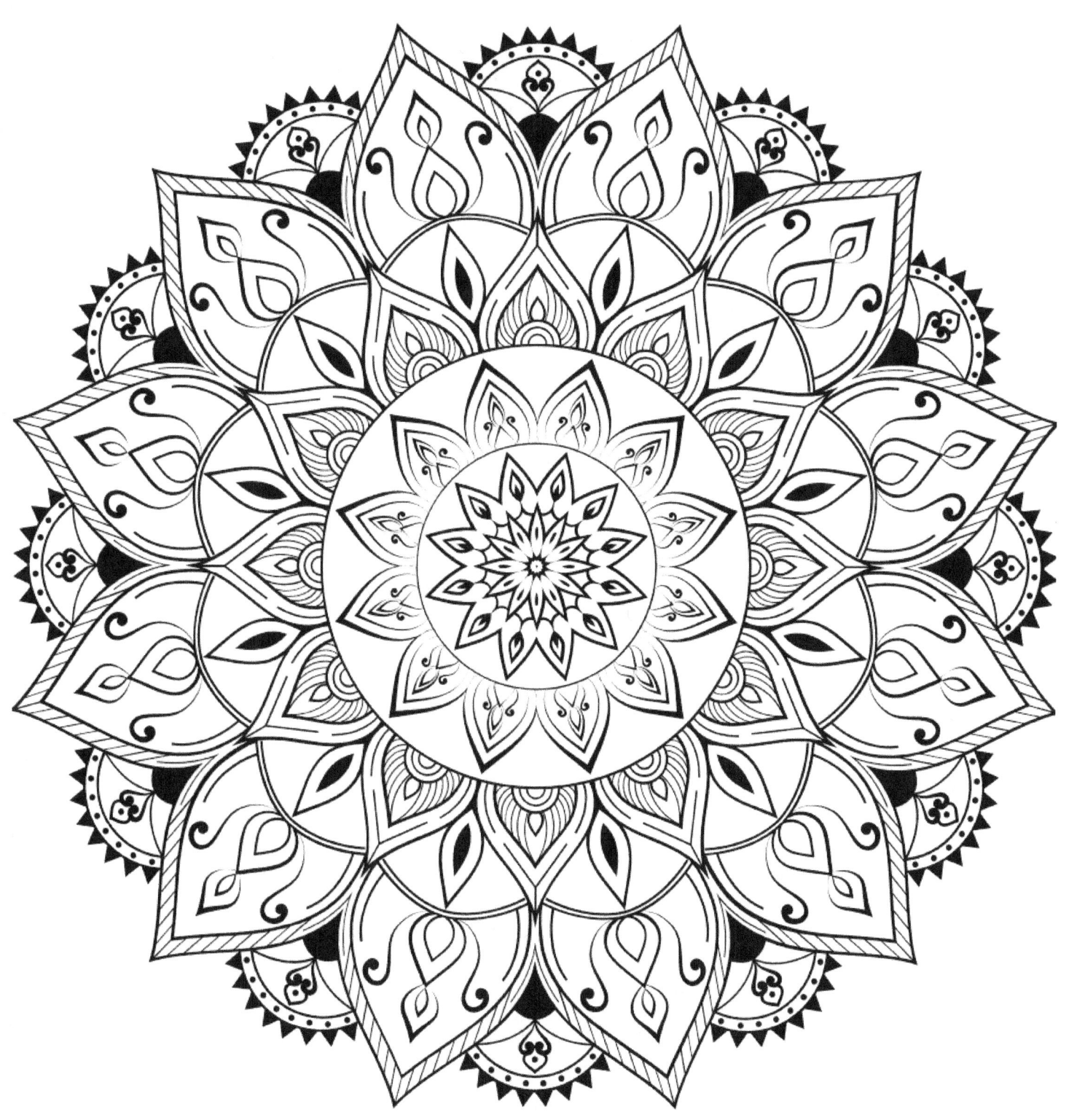

"Embrace the beauty of imperfection; it's the cracks where the light shines through."

- Unknown

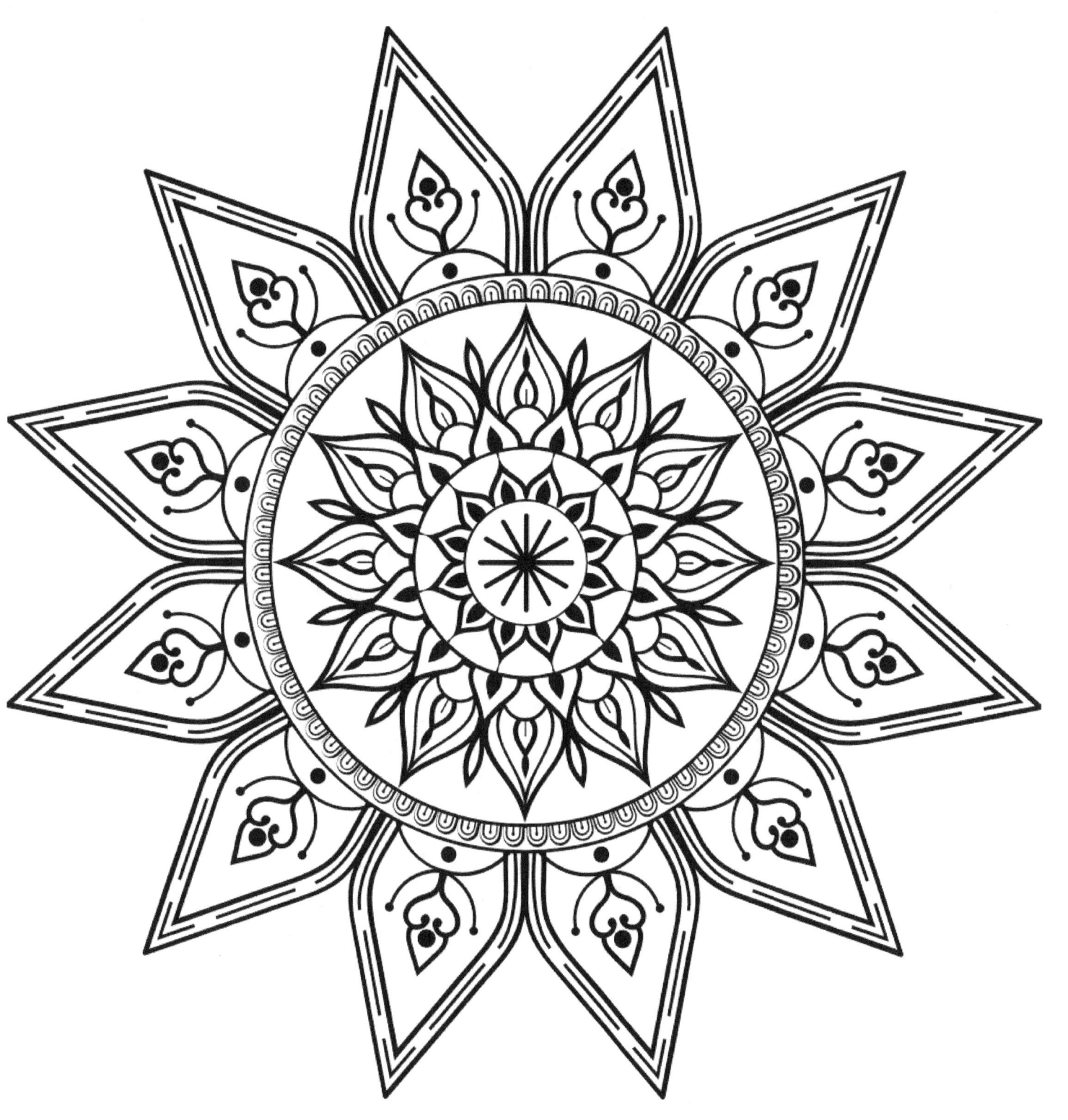

"Inhale confidence, exhale doubt. You are stronger than you know."

- Unknown

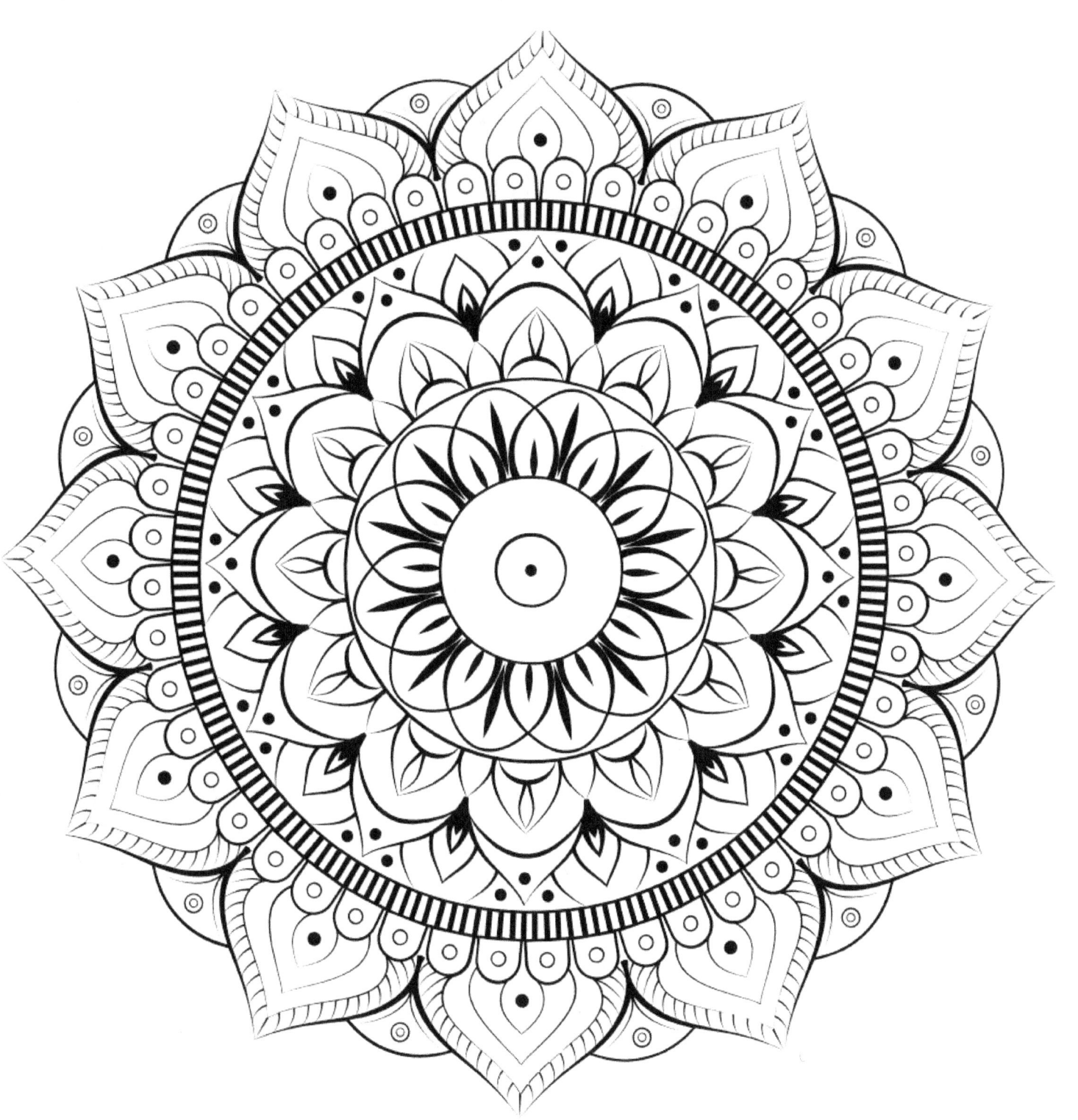

"Find peace in the stillness of your mind, for within it lies the universe."

– Unknown

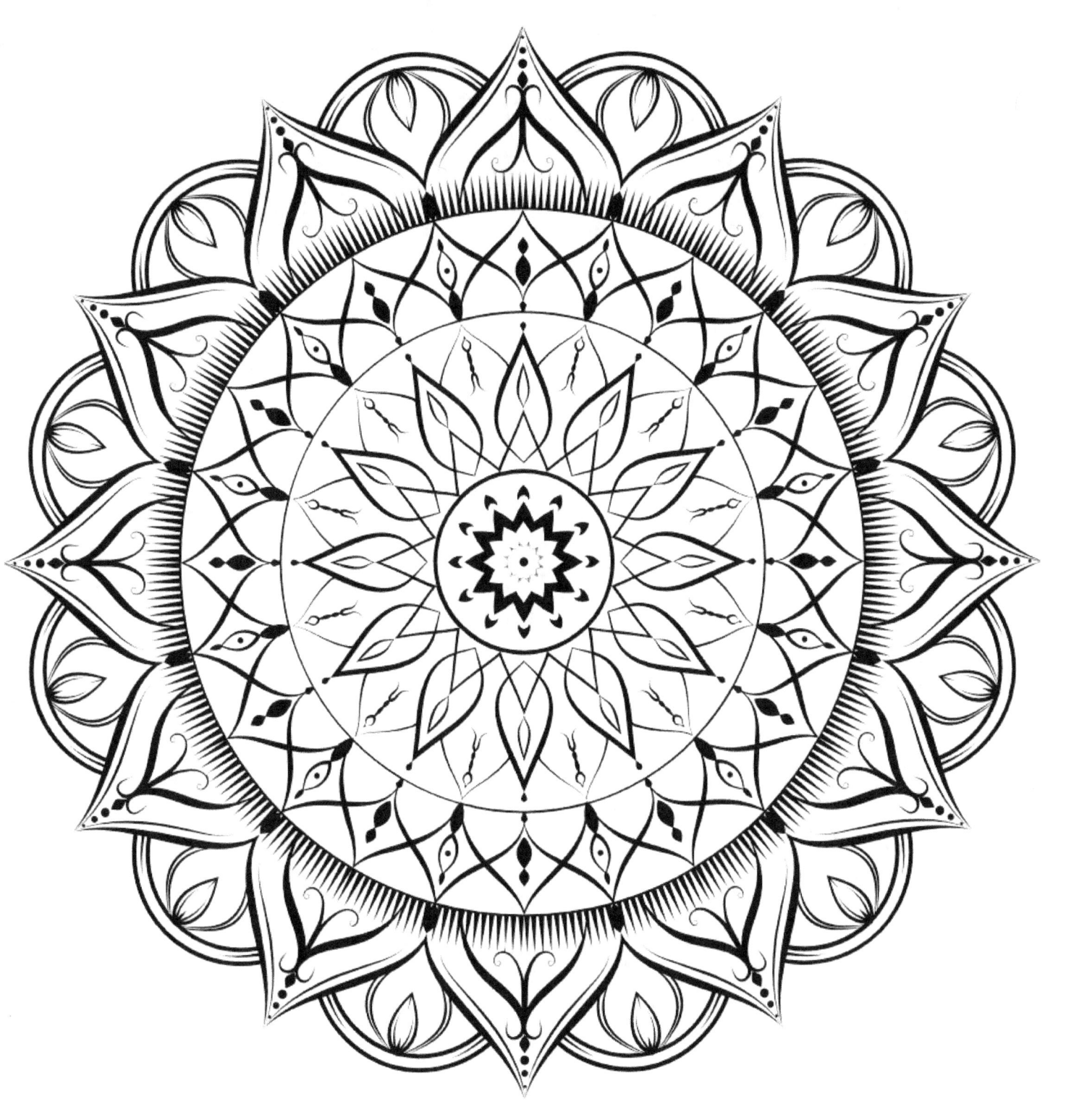

"May your dreams be as wild as the ocean and as vast as the sky."

– Unknown

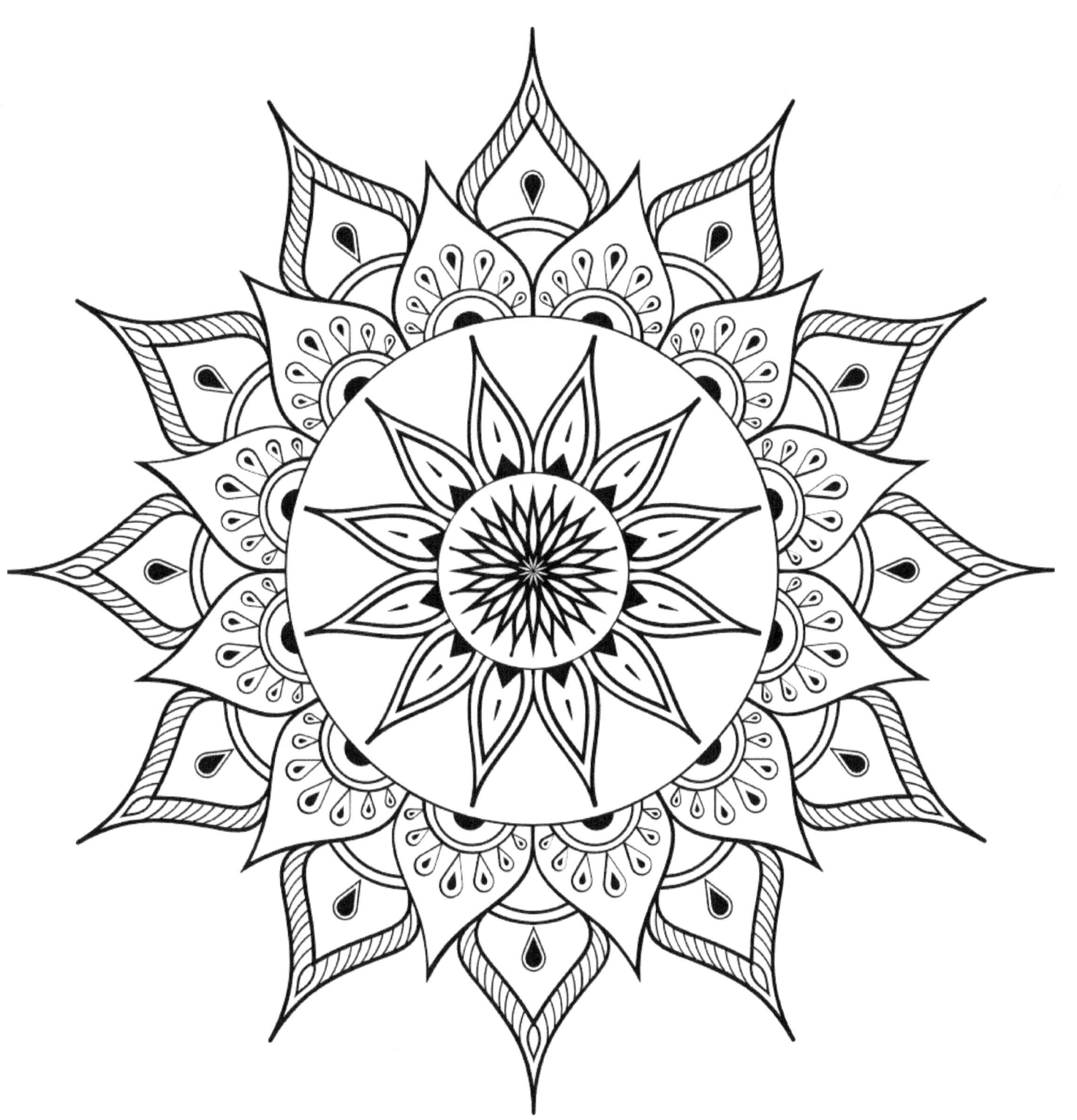

"Plant seeds of kindness and watch as they grow into forests of love."

- Unknown

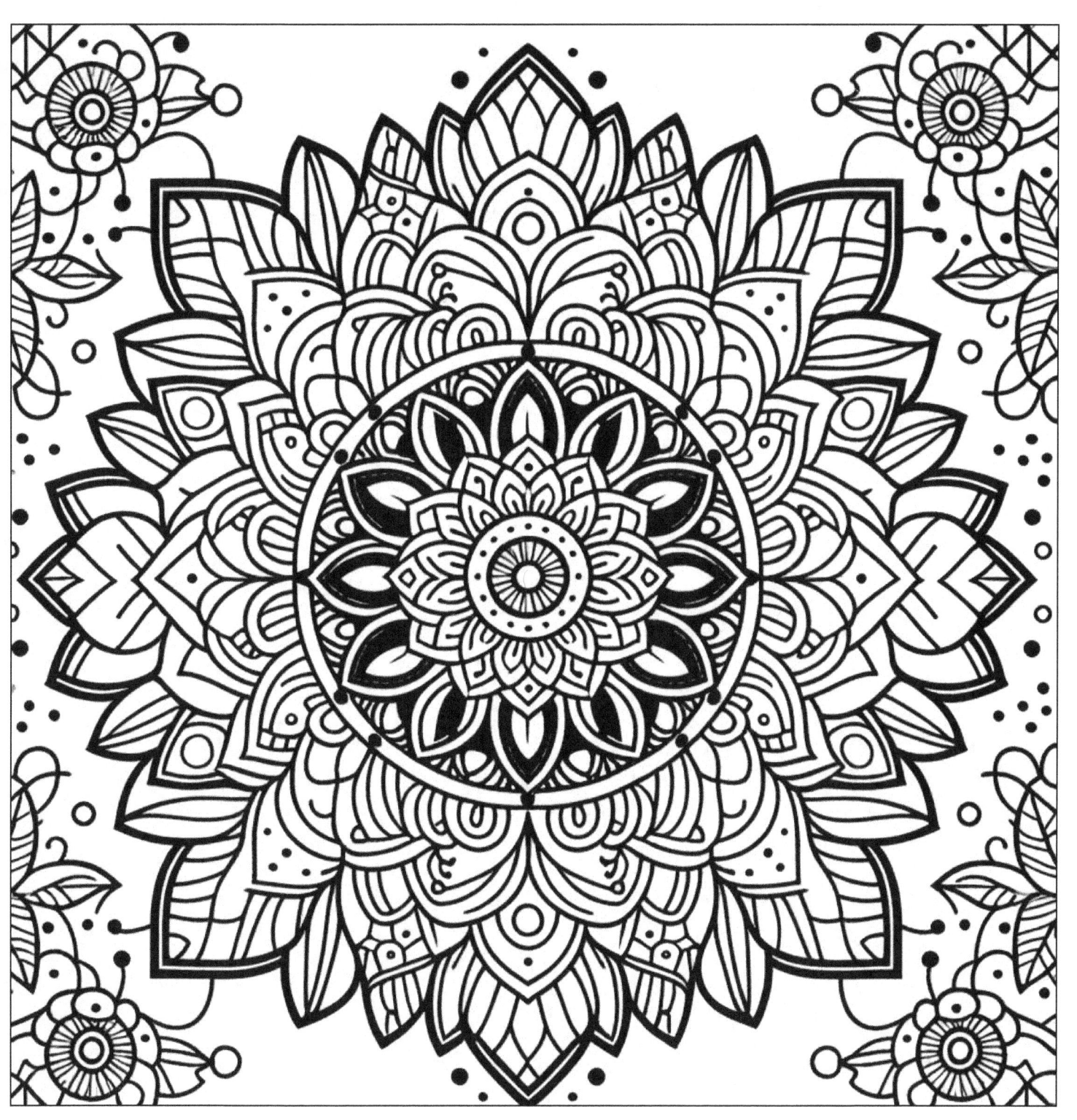

"Life is a symphony; find harmony in the cacophony."

– Unknown

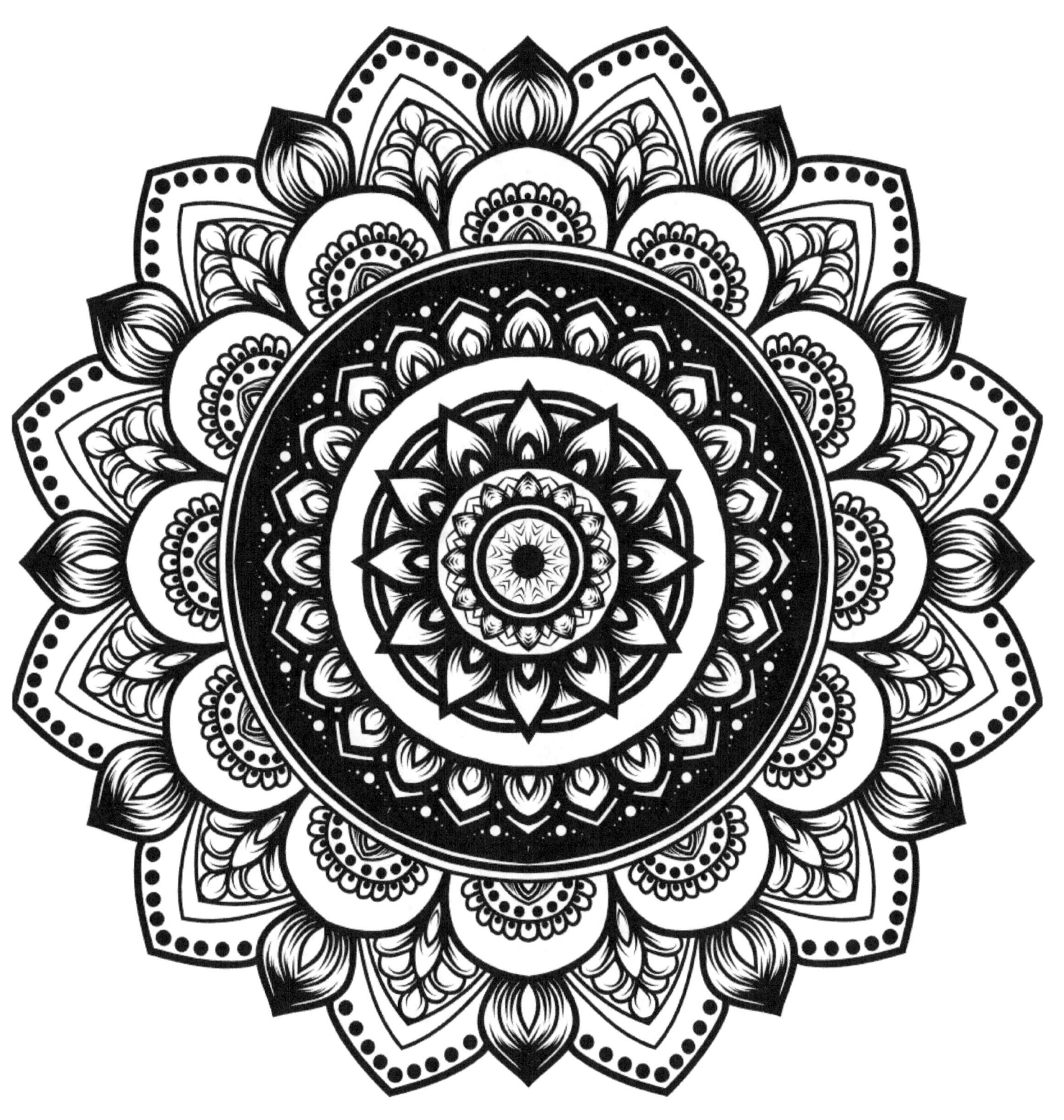

"Let go of what weighs you down and soar with the wings of possibility."

– Unknown

www.ingramcontent.com/pod-product-compliance
Lightning Source LLC
Chambersburg PA
CBHW062223220526
45471CB00009B/3318